Copyright © 2020 Bridgette Freeman
ISBN: 978-1-7377481-9-9

www.kidtoceo.com

All rights reserved. No portion of this book may be reproduced mechanically, electronically, or by any other means, including photocopying, without permission of the publisher or author except in the case of brief quotations embodied in critical articles and reviews.
It is illegal to copy this book, post it to a website, or distribute it by any other means without permission from the publisher or author.

Limits of Liability and Disclaimer of Warranty
The author shall not be liable for your misuse of the enclosed material.
This book is strictly for informational and educational purposes only.

Warning – Disclaimer
The purpose of this book is to educate and entertain. The author and/or publisher do not guarantee that anyone following these techniques, suggestions, tips, ideas, or strategies will become successful. The author and/or publisher shall have neither liability nor responsibility to anyone with respect to any loss or damage caused, or alleged to be caused, directly or indirectly by the information contained in this book.

Cover & Book Design By
Custom Made For You • www.custommadeforyou.net

# C.E.O.
# CHILD ~ ENTREPRENEUR ~ OWNER

This book is dedicated to my amazing husband, Edwin, plus our uniquely and wonderfully made children, Amber and Brayson. They have invested more time listening to this burgeoning idea than it took to complete it. Along with my loving mother, Barbara for providing unwavering support and mother-in-love, Cynthia for being a consistent cheerleader. My village allows me to be my very best and I am forever grateful.

# contents

| | | |
|---|---|---|
| Preface | | 7 |
| Introduction | | 11 |
| Chapter 1 | Knowledge is Power | 15 |
| Chapter 2 | Business Mindset | 19 |
| Chapter 3 | C.L.E.V.E.R. Characteristics | 29 |
| Chapter 4 | Back to Business… Lemonade Business | 43 |
| Chapter 5 | Where Do I Start? | 49 |
| Chapter 6 | Implementing the Steps | 57 |
| Chapter 7 | Create a Business Plan | 81 |
| Chapter 8 | Are Entrepreneurs Born or Bred? | 85 |
| Chapter 9 | Lessons Learned in Business | 93 |
| Chapter 10 | Work Ethic | 97 |
| Chapter 11 | No Fear | 99 |
| Chapter 12 | Problem Solving | 105 |
| Chapter 13 | Develop Patience | 117 |
| Chapter 14 | How Important is Credit? | 123 |
| Chapter 15 | Featured Kidpreneurs | 127 |

Bridgette Freeman

# Preface

It's been said that if you change the environment, you change the person. Have you heard the story of the elephant that would not break free from his rope? The author is unknown, but the story goes as follows. While my friend was walking past a congregation of elephants, a nagging thought caught his attention. He stopped, lost in thought, as he realized the fact that these huge creatures were being held by just a small rope tied to their front legs was inexplicable. No chains, no cages in sight. It was obvious that the elephants could break away from the ropes they were tied to at any time, but for some reason, they did not. My friend saw the trainer nearby and asked why these beautiful, magnificent animals just stood there without making an attempt to escape. "Well," he said, "when they are very young and small, we use the same strength of rope to secure them. And at that age, it's enough to hold them back. As they grow, they are conditioned to believe they cannot break away. They simply have a belief that the rope can hold them, so they never try to break free. It is amazing to think that animals like these can at any time break free from their bonds, but because they believe they cannot, they are stuck in place like monumental statues. Just as in the case of the elephants, I will ask you personally:

how many of us go through life hanging on to a belief that we can't do something because of seemingly insurmountable obstacles? The answer is clear. Limitations exist first in the deep recesses of our minds, and the body follows.

Our past environment and conditions shape our thinking in the present. If a child is told he is too big or small, too fat or skinny – regardless of how the reality of how that statement may change – in his mind's eye, he will see himself with that same "blueprint."

The reverse is true, as well. If you consistently tell a child that she is smart, beautiful, powerful, perhaps a business owner… then she is more likely to believe those affirmations. Why? Your satisfaction or discontent with your loved one is demonstrated with your words and deeds. Whether the object is to convey empowerment or fear, children believe what is articulated and doubly believe what is modeled for them. (How has your self-talk been lately?) The good news is, it's never too late to choose encouragement. Children embrace positive declarations when given the chance.

Yes, I know you may be saying to yourself, "Let's not get carried away here or make things too complicated. This sounds like a lot of work." Surely, the bevy of duties making one a responsible parent would commonly include: listen, be present, be an example, safeguard your child, set boundaries, raise caring kids, promote self-sufficiency and help him become a productive member of society.

Fostering entrepreneurial characteristics might seem like overkill in our modern-day culture of endless appointments, sports and activities. However, I am here to give you valuable tools to fulfill your requirements and additionally move from survive to thrive, even within the confines of limited time to teach lessons.

Rather than be reactive to negative notes about your child's behavior, be proactive and put some "meat on the bone" when it comes to the parental fare you dish out. This is one of the best ways to use real life examples at your child's level, including several movements that can create one demonstrative symphony, encapsulating many of these parental tasks and putting you in front of your goals to provide children with meaningful opportunities. Through your forethought and planning, she can become progressive and self-reliant in a way that includes more engagement and less mindless repetition on your part regarding the values you most want for your children.

This is a practical guide to developing young, successful business owners. It is my hope that these tools will give you the power to develop the next generation of forward-thinking leaders.

Bridgette Freeman

# Introduction

Growing up as an only child in an average working-class family, we didn't have the finer things in life, but we had all we needed. With roots first planted in Michigan and later in New York, concrete pavements gave way to the warmth of community and some sense of freedom. Kids could play outside all day, walk to the corner store, hang out at the local parks and playgrounds or splash around at the swim center. In this way, a sense of play was valued and children could be children in the best sense – exploring, working out ideas, forming relationships. The fun days ended when the streetlights came on.

Injected into the ebb and flow of childhood, I felt an ingrained sense of initiative and responsibility. As a pint-sized business owner of a "diner," (I no longer eat at them, ironically) I would come out with my apron and take orders, preparing the food in the kitchen with care. I had different accents based on the origin of the cuisine on my crafted menu. At closing, I counted the earnings to determine how much money I made that night. Who knew, at my tender age, that I was playing "entrepreneur?"

By the time I entered high school, my sense of freedom of childhood evaporated with my parents' divorce. All our worldly possessions were sold or simply left behind. My mother, a new single parent, and I moved to Georgia with our clothes and an iron. Moving from place to place, high school for me was uneventful and included too many different schools to get my footings established. Still, I managed to become involved in Future Business Leaders of America (FBLA) and served as an officer. Yep, you guessed it, treasurer – I like money! Upon entering college, I took career placement tests which, rather than narrowing down fields of occupation, conversely revealed that I had too many interests. I was left confused about my path moving forward. Although I was interested in the medical profession, I had an inclination, or a nudging that I couldn't quite qualify at the time, to study business. That young Bridgette inside was rooting for me and just knew I would become a business owner.

By the time I had children of my own, enterprising roots had taken hold in a multitude of challenges, notably becoming the youngest female vice president for a Fortune 100 company. Corporate America was not my final destination, as my purest form of entrepreneurship did not flourish even as I was breaking through the glass ceiling. Taking on a supporting role in my husband's business showed that we could do this together, and we later purchased a bakery. The entire family worked every weekend at the bakery. We had many late nights literally "filling" those corporate orders, and we spent time creating beauty in edible art to reflect those glowing expectant mothers. We helped celebrate wins with sports enthusiasts, played practical jokes with goofy co-workers, mark milestones with kids' birthday parties and acknowledged the march of time with adult birthday parties. We sent well-wishes to military servants, encouraged with get-wells and everything in between. It was trial by fire, running a bakery. To keep the engine going at full-throttle, I attended cake decorating classes, designed a website with appropriate holiday updates, reconciled the books, performed opening and closing, all while working a full-time job. A recession hit and we were closed a year later. However, there are no accidents in this world. Operating a bakery full of life – and putting our full lives into our businesses – has taught me many valuable lessons.

In a moment of honesty, most of us would like to make cash fast… and a lot of it. This book does not provide the proviso of an effortless key to a get rich quick scheme. As an aside, even those involved in dishonorable (and illegal) dealings must have honorable entrepreneurial characteristics in order to be successful. The takeaway is, the drive to become a business owner as a trait is not to be confused with the proper skill set, or an honorable business hustle. This includes resilience, hard work and a willingness to evolve. The premise is to educate our young people about the principles of business. A child who understands the basic principles of owning and operating a business develops confidence, giving way to greater successes and a willingness to take quality risks in other areas of life. These principles can be taught and nurtured as lessons that will be remembered for a lifetime.

I recall a stellar example of taking a child's deep desire and putting principles like these beneath as a foundation in a way that demonstrates how to get one's wishes fulfilled in the most satisfying way. As I watched a daytime talk show, the host told a story of a turning point in her teens, as she declared to her father what she wanted for her birthday. Her father listened attentively. But instead of bringing home the sparkling prom dress or the shiny sports car served to her on a silver platter, her father produced huge jars of pickles and a plethora of packaged candy. She tentatively thanked him but asked why he purchased the goodies. He responded that she was going to be the proud owner of a new business as the neighborhood candy girl.

At first confused, she listened as he laid out the framework of how she could sell the items for a profit. Half of the money would be used to purchase additional inventory, while the other half of the profits could be used to buy not just one dress, one time… but continue to provide a way for her to get what she wanted through her own effort. As she recalled this invaluable lesson and reflected on her success, she saw how the principles which allowed her to have financial independence on a small scale when she was young have endured in her adulthood on a much larger scale. This talk show host has multiple businesses and revenue streams, yet attributes her success to those foundational roots that took hold in the form of basic entrepreneurial lessons. It begs the question, why spend money on things for kids rather than spend on what can become true wealth in the form of life lessons that can be passed down through generations? Let's encourage our children to get both a good education and encourage the practical skills of entrepreneurship.

# Chapter 1
# Knowledge is Power

> *"Knowledge is boundless, but the capacity of one man is limited."*
> Chinese Proverb

As humans, we have a tendency to focus on our differences, instinctually searching for our individuality and finding our "tribes." Upon reflection though, one can see that we are much more alike than different. For example, parents want many similar things for their kids. On a very basic level, we want our kids to be happy, healthy and positive contributors to society. We also want to raise them in a safe, loving, supportive environment – and if we're honest – we simply want them to have more opportunities and a better life than ourselves.

In order to accomplish that goal, we must impart values to foster good behavior, good grades, forward thinking and athletic achievement in the early years – just to name a few of these juggling pins! We must pour into our kids the good stuff that yields results, with as much intentionality as we can muster. And, it counts. How many times have you heard an athlete at the pinnacle of their success pay homage to mom, dad or a coach who believed in them? The breeding ground for success is to reach deep into your experience and speak life into your children, encouraging those first models of success that they will experience while under your wing.

Whether it's athletic pursuits or in academia, we give advice like...

> *"Do it once, do it right."*

> *"Glean from others who have accomplished the goals you want to accomplish."*

> *"Practice makes perfect."*

Those nuggets of truth, delivered piecemeal when opportunities arise through the parenting journey, become the building blocks to success. The willingness to show up as a parent despite having workplace and household duties is what makes parenting challenging and also beautiful. It can be the simple things that mean the most; encouraging words issued in that moment when a child encounters a new obstacle are those that inspire confidence and let our youths know we are there for them.

It has been said that it takes 12 correct executions to make a habit and 10,000 hours to become an expert in a field. Children accumulate those so-called "hours" to become the expert student, business owner or athlete through repetition and practice. To be the best, the fastest and the brightest, a steadfast commitment in continued learning is required. We want to shine and remain competitive in our society. If you and yours are not constantly striving to be better, there is someone else willing to do it; this is just a fact of life. We can apply this same premise to businesses and business ownership. In the classic The Art of War, Sun Tzu states, "Don't depend on the enemy not coming; depend rather on being ready for him." Our children will find competition in life whether we prepare them for it, or not. We can look at this reality from a standpoint of scarcity or proactivity in aiming to inspire the same sort of passion and creative thinking that has created the economic atmosphere we have today. This same atmosphere has produced the fertile soil of opportunity and innovation that we can appreciate as such a positive resource.

Allow this book to be a foundational building block for learning about business ownership and fostering creative thinking for the child in your life. The tree of learning is planted now; the work begins with you: the parent, the aunt, the uncle, cousin or leader who cares about the future generations. If you had the fortitude to pick up and start reading this book, but you don't have anyone in your immediate family that shows this type of support, be encouraged. God has and will always put people (hint: and resources) in your path to support and bless you. Remember, you will accomplish a goal in your mind with your drive and vision before it happens in reality. So, examine your mindset as you read and connect with your gratitude. We can be thankful and know that we have quite a lot of power to effect change because of every resource of mind and body which have been presented to us as tools to move forward. You can do so from a place of abundance.

I watched a movie starring Morgan Freeman as a professor who spent years studying the human brain. His character said we have two choices regarding knowledge; we can either pass it on to the next generation, or we are ultimately destroyed with this knowledge kept to ourselves. Great things exist in the pages of books. They allow the information to be transferred and transformed into something new in the mind of the reader. Authors like Napoleon Hill and Dennis Kimbro, who wrote one of my favorites, Think and Grow Rich, are forward thinkers.

I was amazed to find out that the original publication for this work was in 1939. The book's content is still appropriate, generations later. The book empowers you to think differently, practice your craft and work hard so that eventually the fruits of your labor will manifest. This premise can be utilized at any age, and parents have the awesome opportunity to recognize talent and instill the foundations of vision in today's youths. Knowledge is power!

I thought I was a terrible writer until my freshman year English professor said she enjoyed my writing style, and that I should consider English as a college major. What a revelation to me! It was this affirmation that gave me the confidence to know I had something to say, something to give to the world – and that I could be a good writer. The same is true with your kids. When you see your child has a natural interest or talent, use an eagle-like gaze to recognize and hone those abilities. Encourage the child in your life to develop them. It is important, here, to remember to use the spark of his own interests and look for opportunities to build on them. Be intentional about teaching children entrepreneurial characteristics and incorporate them in the early planning stages in this way to gain his buy-in.

This practical guide can be applied to children, teens and young adults. It's never too late to learn and grow. Adults can also benefit from what they are instilling in their children. You will also be strengthened and built up in your resolve by learning about the featured "kidpreneurs" and their parents, knowing how children used their entrepreneurial endeavors to achieve great things at a young age. Get ready to be moved and inspired by their stories!

## Chapter 2
## **Business Mindset**

> *"Don't just leave a legacy. Teach your child to build a legacy."*
> B. Free

Webster defines an entrepreneur as one who organizes, manages and assumes the risks of a business or enterprise. The word entrepreneur is sometimes used loosely, as if building a thriving business is easy to accomplish. To the contrary, by moving outside the cushy model of the employment-type atmosphere to being one's own boss, we typically work the hardest as a business owner.

On the sunny side of this equation, the potential for growth as a business owner is up to you – including potential income – and it is the most rewarding and fulfilling knowing you have built your own castle. In business and in parenting, our sacrifices in time and energy early on will bear much fruit in ultimate rewards for your family. Lessons imparted to children regarding business ownership early in life are just so profitable because kids have no preconceived notions about the nature of business.

Young people also can't conceptualize the risks and possible pitfalls of business ownership as easily as adults. You are dealing with a clean, optimistic slate and can properly emphasize the extreme potential for reward, setting expectations about risk after that is well-established. The Bible talks about having "childlike faith." In learning to take measured risks in youth, one has no reason to believe that it's more probable for the given business to be unsuccessful, so you operate on the side of abundance, as if it IS going to work.

For most children, if they have an interest in accomplishing something, they just do it. The inhibitions that cause us to fear risk are not as evident in the toddler that jumps off your furniture (to their likely physical defeat). The retail giant Nike probably coined the "Just Do It" motto in observing the carefree and optimistic nature of a child. In practice, you may tell your child the basic strategy to be used and, when it is explained in an age-appropriate manner, he or she can begin implementing this plan instantly while under your trusting guidance.

Conversely, maturity brings more rationalization and the additional years of life experience many times will manifest fear and hesitation. Critical thinking skills develop, and those reasoning skills can result in doubts. To be clear, not every child will be excited to start and complete a running business. With a multitude of learning styles and personality traits at play, there may be some reservations or complaining that takes place. When and if this occurs, the main idea is to return to creating a fun and age-appropriate learning process. Remember, teaching entrepreneurship is a totally different mode than our institutionalized education system uses to train our kids to merely fulfill expectations.

It's likely that you would never think to tell a child, "How about you go work on a business plan, just get back to me when it's done." Whoa – what an unreasonable expectation; taking the whole pie at once instead of bite-by-bite. However, expecting a child to perform simple, carefully selected tasks to run a business helps to eliminate the entitlement perspective that many youths develop. This perspective forms in the absence of knowing what adults do to produce money. It also brings to mind the old idiom, "Money doesn't grow on trees." (Neither do iPhones – feel free to quote me on that.)

Giving your child some avenues for practical application to demonstrate the value of hard work is a foolproof way to prevent that disconcerting picture of the 29-year-old adult child eating potato chips on your couch next to a pile of video games… with no real purpose in sight.

Unfortunately, reality TV and social media set an unreasonable bar for young people. The Kardashians of the world measure their success in life by followers, likes and hashtags. The portrayal of a reality star's life is as glamorous as it is easy; they float through red carpet events on the arm of the latest star, decked out from head-to-toe in the latest designer fashions.

The result for our kids is that gaining material things and in-a-flash mega status becomes the goal instead of being empowered to be game changers. There is more to be had than impressing others with your looks and arm candy. Staying authentic and blazing your own trail while being a positive influence bring much more "wealth" to our human experience, ultimately. Learning to taking the road less traveled requires consistency and tenacity. Empowering our kids to be the pioneering entrepreneur versions of themselves will provide them a great sense of achievement, which cannot be taken away.

An article about two teenage girls and their nascent cosmetic company appeared in a local business publication, recently. As I absorbed their story, it seemed the impetus for this company was their mother's entrepreneurial spirit, having herself gained experience at her parents' grocery store. She wisely decided to pass along the great lessons of entrepreneurship learned in her youth. Her daughters started a lip balm company and made $70,000 in sales from online orders at 13 and 14 years old. Within three years, they were picked up by a major retailer with a million dollars in projected sales on the horizon. Can you say college fund? This tells us clearly, entrepreneurship can start at any age.

As stated earlier, our blueprints used later in life come from the environment of our primary family. We soak up the behaviors, practices and attitudes that our caregivers exhibit, whether good or bad. A dynamic hair salon owner recently spoke about her experience of business ownership in her early 20s. She wasn't the soft spoken, slow-to-wrath person that she is today. In her words, she was a hell raiser, albeit a very successful one.

When her first-born son was merely 2 years old, she heard him utter a curse word. The fact that he knew how to say and use this word correctly was surprising and embarrassing. She realized that her children had been imitating her behavior when she started letting slips like these into her daily interaction. When an outside negative experience caused her to curse and fuss, her child learned from that behavior as a result. By the time her next son was born, she was praying, studying and reading her Bible; this was a huge contrast.

Her youngest – seeing her new behaviors and habits – emulated the study of his own Bible. Her examples equally planted seeds in her children, whether positive or negative. Every form of life adapts to its surroundings, even a plant. If you neglect to give a plant water, sun or light it will eventually wither and die. Now, in your mind's eye, capture a photo of that same plant when just one leaf is remaining… withering from lack of care.

If you change its environment, the same plant will produce as if it were never neglected, and the image changes to a thriving organism before your eyes, bursting with new buds of growth. Be that example for the child in your life; it will provide such nourishment to your children. Teaching by example speaks volumes to the children in your life over simply telling a child about the virtues of business ownership.
Perhaps you need to act on a business or product idea, yourself, so that you can be that person in a child's life. This concept may be new to you, as well! To begin examining your own mindset,

try a different way of thinking about your goals. Visualize yourself accomplishing the goal, a huge smile across your face as you explain how well things are going with your business to family and friends (get creative in all the details), and then begin crafting your plan.

The benefits of implementing the steps as described above are twofold. As a parent, you will be teaching as you are learning, which is one of the best ways to really solidify the message for both parties. Hopefully, you will begin applying more of these principles in both professional and personal areas of your life. Success is not determined by your current circumstances!

If you wish that you had more forward-thinking examples early on and feel that you could have achieved more with them in your life, know that your comebacks can be much greater than any setbacks. This happens when you take ownership of your outcomes. And congratulations for wanting to help give a hand "up" to the next generation. While you may not have had every advantage, you do possess a service-attitude that is a huge asset in entrepreneurship. For others, being in business for yourself can be a creative outlet. You may already have a corporate job that you love. However, a side business can be a great outlet and stress-reliever.

In either case, you had an inkling to be the change in the life of a child for a reason. As you become the example to foster business ownership in your children, your child will have a living, breathing testimony to draw from. Knowing that you were personally able to pick up a can-do attitude to achievement in business. Ideas presented here are birthed by simply finding a solution to a problem; easy as that.

Children develop a business-owner mindset by seeing owners creatively addressing potential customers' needs. They will be taught to be the creators and authors of their own story. While you will not expect a child newly introduced to the ideas of entrepreneurship to write the story from beginning to end, you can still prompt some critical thinking in the planning stages. Develop this story by asking your child about the problem (or business need) and what she thinks is a solution. This will help her gain motivation about being involved in the process because you will be saying to her, "Your ideas are important. You can do this."

A retired educator told me she taught her children all issues in life can be approached with the same formula. Recognize the problem, develop the solution and determine strategies and means to get there. She explained that every personal or professional scenario requires the same steps. Recognizing the problem is the important first step; just the simple realization that there is a problem. Determining possible solutions is reasoning and creative thinking, while tackling the problem by executing the chosen solution is the implementation.

In business, a problem need not be negative. In fact, it is an opportunity to the young enterprising mind! Perhaps a young observer (do you have one of those, who never jumps in right away...) notices repeated squabbles at the lunchroom tables at school. Upon closer inspection, the observer sees that Tony always has Little Gizmo snack cakes, we'll call them. Sirena and Robbie sometimes try to trade their various goodies for Tony's Little Gizmo cakes, but lately he hasn't wanted to trade. And our young observer has noticed that others are starting to get involved as well. Tony traded his cakes a few times, but now he has been looking pretty worried as more kids have started to become interested each time lunch break rolls around. He seems a bit jumpy even, with kids reaching around him and touching his carefully packed foods.
Our young observer has recognized a problem! Might an enterprising mind brainstorm a solution to this problem, perhaps deflecting attention from Tony's snack cakes to an even tastier

homemade treat? And, might there be a little extra something in there for our observer, for his or her efforts?! Our observer could look at the "market" and determine what might be most attractive. Could it be cupcakes, iced cookies or perhaps, brownies? Creative problem solving has been deployed. Once the preferred solution is determined, it will be time to implement. Perhaps our young observer even has a built-in spokesperson.

Tony, no doubt eager to shed his recent lunchtime popularity, might be keen to be the first to suggest that his "friends" try an alternative to his lunch: our young observer's new lunchtime treats. There also will be logistical factors to work out such as baking times and distribution – and even school policy politics to navigate – in the execution of the plan.

The lesson I teach my kids first and foremost, is to make good choices. My daily affirmation to my kids is to 'have a great day, love you and make good choices.' Good choices are encouraged in all three steps of the described problem-solving process. It is a choice to recognize and accept a problem (how often have people in your life been less-than-willing to accept when they had an issue?), work thoroughly on finding a solution and in the thought process.

One can also make good choices when implementing a business plan, by showing grit once encountering inevitable obstacles. By continuing to adjust and evolve your plan of action as you respond to the market around you, your good choices will yield results. It's not the adversity that arises which is the point of the lesson for young and old alike, but how you respond to it.

In business, there will always be challenges. No matter the age, a business owner feels empowered when each goal is accomplished; making a profit is icing on the cake. It is the same reason that some parents keep their children involved in sports activities. There is a sense of accomplishment for the child who trains, prepares and works collectively on a team. Each of these tasks provides a lesson and gives the athlete a small 'win.' Collectively, these small wins build confidence. It is most helpful, however, as a lesson when an athlete experiences victory or major goal is accomplished. Not only is it validation that she is a great athlete, but that hard work can bring meaningful rewards. Medals or trophies provide further validation.

My daughter and her best friend started a jewelry business when they were 15 years old. Although the business was operating for just for one year, my daughter learned a great deal about business operations and communication skills in a partnership with her co-owner. Even more, she exuded confidence and had a chance to tackle obstacles that came her way.

Under light guidance, she felt confident in her ability to make good choices to change her own circumstances. You might be asking, where and how do you begin to inspire a child when you might need inspiration, yourself? Well, you can learn along with your children. These instructions are your arsenal. Again, implement the steps with your children and their courage will inspire you to continue!

As a note, imparting the lessons of a business owner, or having an enterprising mind, do not necessarily mean establishing a business. Although my goal is that you and your child are encouraged to start a business, the more important concept is thinking like a visionary.

Entrepreneurial habits include high-level communication, goal setting, implementing a plan, thinking outside the box, delegating and determining how to make money from your vision, just to name a few. Most adults figure out this process in a more protracted way years after school is finished. Instilling child-sized bites of these traits will further develop and have lasting ripple effects into adolescence and adulthood.

This will allow the child in your life to tackle challenges with more confidence. Kidpreneurship has the same effect as a child that thrives in sports or excels academically. You can help plant the seed and create the feeling that anything can be accomplished, which is a wonderful outlook for a young person to start with as she is presented with more independence and greater decision-making as time goes on.

Bridgette Freeman

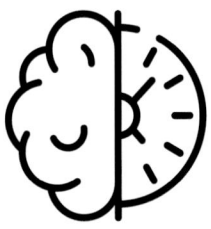

# Chapter 3
# C.L.E.V.E.R. Characteristics

> *"Logic will get you from A to B. Imagination will take you everywhere."*
> Albert Einstein

These are six basic steps to develop entrepreneurial characteristics in a child. After all, children are clever. An entrepreneur must be creative, a leader, energetic, a visionary, an effective communicator and resilient – **C.L.E.V.E.R.**

Let's inspect each quality from this acronym.

1. Creative expression
2. Leadership
3. Energetic
4. Visionary
5. Effective Communicator
6. Resilient

**C** is for encouraging **creative expression**. Allow your child to express his ideas without judging. When a child initially says, "I want to sell lemonade," this becomes a teachable moment. That implied query is your chance to start creating a brilliant entrepreneurial mind. Don't miss it! Treat this initial (quite positive) thought as an opportunity to harness a future million-dollar idea.

Help him brainstorm and expound it. How confident do you think your child will become when you express an interest in what he does, when you help him take his own ideas and run with them? Continue to brainstorm with your child on his business or product idea, asking realistic questions.

You would ask questions about the lemonade stand. For example, to whom will he sell the lemonade? What are all the things you need to make lemonade? And how much do lemonade mix, sugar, cups and napkins cost? You are asking the questions so that your child can take a stab at working things out for himself. Even if your child is clumsy, forgetful or disorganized – it doesn't mean he cannot be an effective business owner. Quite frankly, CEOs hire the best people who chiefly support the mission of the company. We all have shortcomings, and business owners are no different. Support of a given business comes in various forms, like a parent who's involved in the day-to-day operations. It's an analogy of business structure at large.

The best business owners know how to delegate and ask for support when needed. The definition of critical thinking is the objective analysis and evaluation of an issue to form a judgment. The entire exercise of young entrepreneurship is an opportunity to harness critical thinking. Your child is learning how to handle objections, make connections and form a consensus among partners and supporters. Corporations call this a round table discussion. The process of raising questions and finding the answers is fostering creativity and ideas.

Remember, young children are impressionable. If you believe it, he will believe it too. Conversely, if you are "half-in," your child will be able to sense that hesitation. As a child gets older, keep the same abundance mindset. Don't be moved by outside agents; this will help the child to stay the course, as well. If an older child says he has an idea, he needs you to take up the torch and fan that spark into a flame. Your child, having not seen the outcome and unaware of the very possibility of success, needs to see this through your eyes.

Speak life into the project by talking about how fun it is going to be to plan, prepare and perform the daily tasks that will reap so much reward. You can talk about how you will celebrate when you hit that first goal mark, how you'll both be smiling from ear-to-ear, sitting on top of the world. That you will be able to say that you did it, together, with the goal coming from the heart of the child who created it all. Generating some emotions around success at the beginning will help set the stage by going in with a winning outlook (and, will ultimately actually result in more success). Again, you see the vision first. Then, help him to see the vision.

Before the popularity of the internet and the tunnel vision that arises from electronic devices, children played outside. As a child, we made up games for everything: kick ball, hand ball, stick ball, dodge ball, hand games and hide-and-go-seek. While I lived in the city, I'm sure the kids in the country were catching bugs, fishing, playing in the creek, riding bikes and climbing trees. Exploring life outside in the open air made the world our playground. The activities that children encounter outside foster more creative thinking, release endorphins and allow for natural exposure to Vitamin D. We've lost those activities in the post-electronic generation. These generations must have organized play which, when presented to them like a menu, does not require as much brain power. It's almost as if they can't play unless there are a set of directions.

With pre-designed activities served on a silver platter to children, this blueprint also decreases their overall engagement in play. In this way, they are more likely to lose interest in those over-directed activities and revert back to the world of overstimulation offered by the digital era. Kids still have the capability to be creative, but we must help them to flex and grow these parts of the brain just as with any other muscle by starting early and encouraging creative sparks of genius.

Parents are at fault by choosing the lesser of two evils, perpetuating this state with scheduled play dates. This creates an environment as if there is a referee keeping time; at the end of 45 minutes, the whistle has been blown and the playing must stop. However, when you think about it, playing is their work – and their work is never done. Goodness! Life can be hard enough; let's not destroy playtime, too! Parents and children should be free from the bondage of forced and directed play.

Spontaneity in the task of play goes a long way to build a very different brain. And that is where the fine line has been crossed: playtime is an essential task, but the requirement here is for it to be fulfilled by tasks of organic design. So, they should be allowed to flourish without the fruits of critical thinking having been artificially extracted to compel specific play activities.

Dumping the task of scheduling all aspects of your child's agenda may even free your stress-riddled mind from unneeded tasks and help develop greater balance for your own life. With so much to juggle at home and whatever work is on our plates, most adults in today's society have a need to focus on fewer priorities (and to know the order of said priorities).

Let it go – relax and be creative with your child. These are moments you can never get back. Work will forever be waiting for you. Don't think for a moment in the absence of pressure and overarching structure to direct your children, that society won't offer its own pressures.

In his pre-teen to adolescent years, my son actually put enormous pressure on himself. And it's great that, as an overachiever, he was able to reap much benefit from his self-motivated drive. All kids have different ways to flourish, so for the kids who insist on being their best, you might do well to help them dial back the pressure and have a little fun.

On the other hand, many kids do pretty well in the relaxation department, so in that situation you might consider encouraging more focus. In any case, creativity should be equally celebrated with the overachiever, the analytical over-thinking type and the social butterfly. It can be a great reservoir from which to draw during their life paths and can propel them in later years when you won't be waiting in the wings to assist.

**L** is for **leadership**. It's common for parents to want their kids to be leaders and not default to following at all times. In essence, we are telling them, "Chart your own course; determine what is good for you, personally." Moreover, the statement means be a leader. Each has their own talents and instinctual drives. It's important to help children become their authentic selves by knowing and developing their own gifts. With the freedom to explore, what is natural to one will rise to the surface, where he can then embrace the talent and use it for productive means. An odd characteristic which brings on teasing from peers may become the very thing that makes them different; a uniqueness that helps him stand out from the crowd.

For example, if one is significantly shorter than others at school, the idea of being short might become the object of much anxiety as the child realizes – to her dismay – that she is different from the rest of her class. However, this makes her distinguishable because of her height. She is memorable because people may refer to her as the short basketball player. Teach your kids to look at the glass half-full, not half empty. This brings the situation from being simply short to being "the only short ball-player on the court to make a 3-pointer – and how cool is that!" A self-leader learns to embrace how they are different in a way that they can use to their advantage.

The goal is to be the best you that you can be. However, don't confuse conforming, following rules and respecting authority with not being a leader. A leader is a person that is respected, admired and is someone whom others want to take direction from naturally. It's about the confidence to be a leader in any capacity.

Furthermore, another opportunity for you to shine the light on your child comes from the fact that he may not have uncovered his own innate leadership characteristics. A leader is not afraid to be the nerve center for decision making; neither are they reluctant to be the touch point for others to rely upon. They assume responsibility for mistakes and accept the risk that comes with a new undertaking. These are admirable traits in any industry or environment. Each child holds limitless potential.

Unfortunately, the skills can also be misused. A gang leader also has these leadership characteristics. A gang has an organizational hierarchy and a figurehead who is to be followed. There is order, process, there are meetings and even a plan for financial gain. It is unfortunate when those skills are used for selfish means and not to make a positive difference in the world. But this only proves the absolute utility of certain skills. They do work. Leadership can be anywhere; found in organizing sports teams, class projects, club organization and can even be found in the decisions made between siblings in a fight. The lesson is, your kids may find opportunities to flex their leadership muscles in many ways and it is likely that they do not realize their potential.

E is for **energetic**. The definition of energetic is operating with or marked by vigor or powerful effect. The energetic factor means to tackle tasks with a sense of determination. To move a cause in a good direction, this energy needs to be of an optimistic nature – best used when full of hope! So, one must have a good attitude. To illustrate, my husband and I were talking about his recent visit to a favorite sandwich joint. Initially excited to be eating a delicious deli sandwich, within moments he witnessed an exchange between the manager and worker in the back. When the manager asked the worker to handle a task in the lobby, the worker rebuffed by asking, "Why do I have to do this? Couldn't you ask someone else?" The manager was forced to repeatedly assert why she needed him do to it in a tense tone, resulting in a foul-smelling volley back and forth that seemed to curb the delicious fragrance of the deli meat. Others in the restaurant took notice, and it got quiet as the employee cursed and made a scene saying, "This job doesn't pay me enough to take this treatment!" What a terrible attitude – and in front of customers! I don't care if you are responsible for slicing tomatoes and/or cleaning tables; do it with enthusiasm and to the best of your ability. Those who prove themselves trustworthy in the simple matters will be given larger responsibilities. Why? If you are faithful in those small tasks, it is most assured that you will approach the larger, more challenging tasks with just as much gusto and pride in getting the job done.

This demonstrates why shows like Undercover Boss exist. Employers want to know which employees are operating with the right attitude and who are carrying out the mission and goals of the organization. Going through the motions to simply get tasks checked off the list doesn't help customers to have the amazing experience the owner envisioned when the organization was started.

So, the reason why entrepreneurs – and supportive staff at large – succeed is because they accept wise instruction to edify themselves and bring up those around them. Whether you refer to it as good karma, vibes or energy, it contains the same ingredients and it produces results. Others will resonate with the energy of someone who makes them feel good, and likewise will be demoralized by someone with a poor attitude. Positivity is contagious and being energetic promotes that type of synergy among team members.

For each industry, the right type of energy provides the "secret sauce," or X-factor, that makes or breaks success for a career. Entertainers are colorful, vibrant and enthusiastic in performing. Great speakers are enthusiastic in their delivery and passionate about the message. If a speaker in the working world stands with his hands at his sides using a dry, monotone voice, that will likely be the last speech he ever makes. The best salespeople are believable, relatable and convey concern for the choices of those they are helping.

By contrast, if a salesperson is representing a product or service and doesn't completely believe in it, this will be apparent as the non-verbal cues and words used will sound disingenuous to those listening. The general public can "feel" the cover-up and the patchwork used by the representative in their approach to artificially create excitement about the product. Hence, the energy for your cause must be sincere in order to be effective.

**V** stands for **visionary**. Let's take a moment ask ourselves as parents, how are we doing in the category of vision for our children's lives? It can be said that vision is equivalent to having faith, in a sense. You cannot see the business or idea, but there must be a clear picture in your mind before you start. Children are naturally uninhibited and luckily are a great at having vision! They have imaginary friends, use pretend items to build scenarios, creating elaborate role-play characters.

Think about the following scene and consider what your honest reaction would be. Your child says, "Mommy, I want to be a singer," with all the hope of humanity in her eyes. What initial knee-jerk reaction comes to mind? Perhaps for many parents, the internal dialogue would go, 'Hmmmm, but she can't sing, so how do I let her down gently here?' If you tell your child this, you are responding by shutting your child down; you are not allowing the idea to manifest in the mind of the child.

Instead, use this as an opportunity to help develop the process of formulating and implementing a plan. Will the child become a singer? Maybe, or maybe not. But that is beside the point. The child's bright idea becomes a teachable moment in this case. This is not the time to make an overall decision; rather, it is the time to gather information. Make a point to determine her level of interest based on how much detailed information the child has, or if she has considered the possibilities of executing the idea.

In an employment situation, imagine how important it is for business owners to have people in management that believe in the organization's goals, and equally how negative water cooler talk about coming to work "only out of necessity" needs to be eradicated. For the unit to survive and stay together, isn't it just as important to support your family as a team? We need to believe in the mission of lifting our children up. So even if you might have missed the mark in the past, how about embracing the next enterprising idea your child might produce. If the idea is extremely unpalatable (which will be quite rare), at the very least, act as if by asking questions to see what exactly he may be thinking about, in detail.

My son wanted to play tenor saxophone when he signed up for band in middle school. The assignment of each instrument was based on how well the child responded to the various types used on a trial basis, how well they read music and took direction. The music teacher used this unbiased information to make assignments. Compared to the desire the child had for the instrument, it is possible that a child could get sidetracked in thinking about their favorite drum player, and could possibly choose an instrument that does not complement their skills, or for the wrong reasons. My son decided to prove his desire by eating, sleeping and breathing tenor saxophone. He watched instructional videos, talked up its virtues to anyone who would listen and found written lessons for the instrument. He watched videos of artists playing the tenor saxophone night and day, not to mention researching the best places to rent or buy the saxophone. In his mind, he believed he was going to have and play the tenor saxophone. Then, the fateful day came when his music teacher made the announcement. He was assigned the tenor saxophone!

The number one reason that he achieved this victory was that he envisioned himself playing it, and his seat in that chair was as good as assigned already; he believed it as a matter of fact. What others said was of no consequence; he had no reason to think otherwise and his vision literally put that brass instrument right into his hands. Kids have faith and belief. To them, it doesn't matter if is unreasonable, that it's hard or that it has not been done before. What matters is that he wanted it for himself, and was willing to work hard toward the goal. Have enough faith to believe that it can happen.

**E** is for **effective communicator**. I Love Toastmasters International. It is the oldest and largest public speaking organization in the world – yes – the world! The mission is one I adopted for my own children; to develop speakers to become more effective communicators. Think about the amount of communication in your typical workday. You arrive at the office, check emails, make a few calls, follow up on open items, orders, services and the like. After a quick lunch ordering from the kind man at a nearby café, you might have an afternoon meeting and write a memo, before yet more emails and phone calls. The entire day involved communication of some form!

Each activity and movement you made was layered with interpersonal interaction. Hey, maybe you don't have one of those typical office jobs… something else, entirely. Let's imagine a common Saturday agenda. You might get up early to cook breakfast, spend a bit of time with your family, then run errands like going to the gym, bank, post office or grocery store. Perhaps later on, you see that movie you promised the kids, then meet some friends for dinner. Totally different activities – and yet they still involve communication in one form or another.

If you don't leave your house, you may reach out to others via phone, email or social media, as well as work with your family members on chores or around mealtimes. We are always in constant communication, so shouldn't we put thought into something we spend almost all our waking hours doing, and do it well? It doesn't mean you aspire to be a professional speaker… or maybe you do. The idea is to take steps to simply be an effective communicator. What happens if we don't put effort into crafting our messages to others in an effective way?

Take just one area: romantic relationships. I don't need to proceed very far here when speaking about this ultra-close and high impact form of communication before many people can immediately relate. When communication isn't good in your relationship, trouble abounds. From a mis-represented or misread text message, to one party having trouble stating their needs and causing a grain of sand to turn into a mountain… this area clearly takes all the communication skills one can muster. The same communication blunders can also be applied to workplace dynamics and communication with your kids.

High-performing salespeople know how to effectively deliver information and engage the audience. The effectiveness in the message comes in the way it is delivered. An effective salesperson will help you discover the benefits and how the purchase makes sense for you. Customers tend to make emotional decisions and back those up with informational data, filling it in after the fact – whether for or against the ultimate sale. A less effective salesperson tends to accept the potential objections the customer has with the sale, without showing excitement about the possible outcome of owning the product and the emotional side of how much joy it would bring to the customer's life.

Therefore, the ineffective salesperson has simply "laid down" and let objections kill the sale. In order to overcome those objections, the salesperson must have that belief in what they are selling, have the vision and be able to communicate this to the customer. Without this, success will not come easily.

I'll provide another example from raising my own children to illustrate how to help kids have belief in their communication skills when they need to influence others. When they wanted the latest game or device, my kids had to prepare a proposal. Nothing formal on paper, but to know their reasons well, to verbally make the request in a convincing way. For instance, one of my children wanted the latest tablet device. Part of this communication process was to make his case. He had to provide at least three supporting details for the argument; the more reasons, the better. He needed to be able to stand before us confidently, looking us in the eye and showing his unwavering belief that he should be able to gain this new gadget. His reasons would be things like these: he could read on it, play educational games and watch videos. He could entertain himself independently and listen to music. After the case was made, we refrained from giving an opinion or position.

Without flinching or giving him the immediate satisfaction of knowing whether we agreed, we told him we will take his position under advisement and gave a reasonable time frame such as two days to receive the results. This put him in the mindset where he must know that he had done his very best, no matter what we said. After completing this process several times, he learned to be able to sit with the good job he had done in stating his justification for this purchase. You can foster behavior during childhood that teaches kids to ask for what they want confidently.

In order to do this, kids will need to have inspected their reasons for wanting material items, so they can get to know their motivation behind the steps they wish to take in life and proceed with a greater sense of self-awareness and confidence.

Help your child see the vision. Over time she will learn to be decisive, confident and learn persuasive techniques. In a typical real-world scenario at work or in the community, an applicant has just 30 seconds to persuade someone's decision. You have just one opportunity to make a first impression. So, whether it's the lemonade stand or written marketing communication for a teen's personal business, effective communication is key. Communication also helps foster positive relationships with parents, teachers, friends and later in life, employees.

**R** stands for **resilient**, which in practice means relentless persistence. Have you ever witnessed a parent telling their child "no" to a request? What does the child do? They ask again, and again, and again for the same thing – without jumping ahead to predict that if they have received no 15 times in a row, that they might receive the same result once more. They do this with gusto, as if the parent had never said "no" in the first place.

Can you imagine asking for the contract, the job or the internship role over and over again and never expecting to hear "no?" With this trait of resilience, you would ask over again until it turns into a yes. Persistence is a lost art. Don't stop until you get what you want. Be resilient; be steadfast; be determined. Children already embody this trait naturally, while parents have to recall information from the recesses of their uninhibited childhoods to support its development.

We may tell our kids, "Don't give up now… keep going… keep asking… keep pursuing." The best attitude to adopt in business and life is that each no means you are closer to the next yes. Help children to embrace it early on, so a no won't be devastating when it happens. They can best develop resiliency and tough skin to get them through the trials now, because while they have you now, the world has no mercy.

Bridgette Freeman

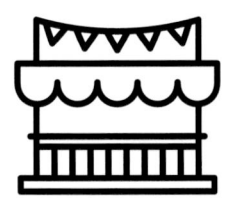

## Chapter 4
## Back to Business… Lemonade Business

> *"When life gives you lemons, make lemonade."*
> Unknown

Owning an entrepreneurial mind does not always result in owning a business. It does mean thinking like a visionary (to include developing entrepreneurial habits like effective communication, goal setting, developing confidence to implement a plan, thinking outside of the box, delegating and realizing profits from this vision.) Most adults figure out parts of this process – piecemeal – years after school, and some never learn. Let's explore these concepts with the lemonade stand example. As a true model of business, each entrepreneurial ingredient is needed here to succeed. It's also a classic example of business in its simplicity.

There are even large organizations based on the lemonade stand! Prior to taking a look at the actual characteristics to be applied (the how), let's first talk about what your child would best understand first (the what.) When your child hangs her sign up and starts doling out the thirst-quenching cups, she will find one pitcher makes 25 cups of lemonade which, sold at $1 each to make it simple; yielding $25 of income. Have her determine what's needed to make lemonade: sugar, water, lemons, cups and napkins. The cost is $2.50 for sugar, $6 for lemons, $2 for cups and $1 for napkins. The total is $11.50 (the expenses). The difference of $13.50 is the net profit.

You explain the math:
- If we sell 25 cups of lemonade at $1 each, we will have $25
- The cost for cups, napkins, sugar and lemonade mix costs $11.50
- $25 (income) - $11.50 (expenses) means we will make $13.50 for each batch of lemonade

---

Congratulations, you have just learned fundamentals of business! I'm going to save you thousands of dollars of college tuition here. The basic premise of business is to buy low and sell high. Television's Shark Tank personality and businessman Daymond John has said that the success of a business is based on two premises: either reduce expenses or increase productivity. In other words, make more money than it costs you to produce it or figure out a way to produce more. A business can only be successful if the income exceeds expenses (otherwise it's a charity!).

Although simple in nature, these simple statements explain the principles of business perfectly. Start with a good model, one with which you can make a profit (sadly, some adult entrepreneurs start their own business with less planning.) When kids are first taught the basics, business becomes easy to understand.

Have the planning conversation with your child. The young entrepreneur in your life has come to you and asked to start a lemonade stand. You're now going to nurture that idea by asking critical questions. Notice in the following example conversation how you can facilitate reasoning and communication.

*Parent/Caregiver:* Why do you want to make the lemonade or sell it?
*Child:* I like lemonade and my friends like lemonade.

*Parent:* Do you think you might want to try selling this for 50 cents or maybe $1?
*Child:* Fifty cents sounds good. I want to sell as much as I can.
*Parent:* Who will we sell the lemonade to?
Child: My friends, neighbors and people outside walking to the park.
*Parent:* What are all the things you need to make the lemonade?
*Child:* We need lemonade mix, lemons, sugar, cups, a big spoon and napkins.
*Parent:* That's good, now if we sell 50 cups of lemonade for 50 cents each, how much money will we make AND how much does the lemonade mix, sugar, cups and napkins cost? (Help him figure it out. Tell him not to worry about the spoon, you will let him have yours.)

In this example, this question and answer process develops critical thinking skills in your child. The communication occurring is how the child is explaining his plans for the business and providing details on how he wants to give it a go.

Let's examine the **C.L.E.V.E.R.** steps as related to the example business: the lemonade stand. You might ask the child to expand their creative vision of the lemonade stand – perhaps, in what other ways could we make the lemonade? You might suggest lemonade slushies or flavored lemonade to get the wheels turning. Entrepreneurs must be creative in their product/service offerings to compete in the business world. The creativity does not stop there; it must continue throughout the business life cycle. What are the latest trends, tips and tricks in the industry? How can you use your creativity to solve logistical issues in the business? Even at the end of the life cycle, creativity is needed to sell or liquidate a business.

Leadership for the lemonade stand example means the child is embracing ownership and can practice some lightly guided decision-making. You are building confidence by letting the child know it's their business. The child decided things like the name, who's going to work at the stand, whether they will have a business partner, how supplies will be provided and what other products might be sold together with the lemonade. They can decide to give a portion of proceeds to a non-profit organization or determine a theme for their stand (or stands!). All final decisions are made by the child; the owner, the entrepreneur. It's empowering that the business went from conceptual to actual and is successful, yielding a profit.

An energetic personality is contagious. This is the lesson to teach a child is being excited about their business. It is so important to respond positively to his ideas, so as not to squash his natural enthusiasm. From having a flashy job in entertainment to becoming the best store clerk there ever was, being excited about the task at hand means more repeat business and overall success. You've heard the saying, "If you love what you do, you will never work again." This goes hand-in-hand with the excitement in that current job or business. Those who pursue what they are excited about – and keep connected to the feeling they had when they first started – can use this to their advantage.

Being a visionary is needed in the lemonade stand business, too. Does your child expect to run the lemonade stand solely in her own town? There's a non-profit organization called the Alex's Lemonade Stand Foundation. The founder was named Alexandra Scott, a 9-year-old who was diagnosed with cancer. She originally started the stands with the money to be donated for cancer research and grew the stands across the state and country! Although she became a lovely angel in heaven, the organization continues to raise money throughout the country for cancer research (more than $18 million to date) and for the families experiencing childhood cancer.

Practice effective communication. Teach children to sell themselves and take a stand when they have an idea. When you made your forte into the lemonade stand business with your child, you asked questions about why they want to sell lemonade, to whom they want to sell it and how much it will cost. The child is learning to form her value proposition about the product and why others might want to buy it. You are birthing qualities that demonstrate the nature of business; people will want to know what she can do for them. You must be able to prove this before you start.

Being resilient simply means staying the course. Don't give up if it rains for a couple days and there are no customers. Being resilient means continuing the process, even if none of the lemonade made for that day sells, or grouchy neighborhood dogs run off your customers. These lessons about persistence will pay off tenfold in many facets of life and business. Never give up when it seems too difficult!

Bridgette Freeman

## Chapter 5
## Where Do I Start?

> *"The journey of a thousand miles begins with one step."*
> Chinese Proverb

The most difficult and most rewarding journeys – be it the founding of Apple, Inc. or building the Great Pyramids of Giza – all have a beginning. Many times, like in the founding of the electronics giant by Steve Jobs and Steve Wozniak, those beginnings can be quite small and humble. The pair started building just one computer in a garage, Jobs having been a formerly directionless college dropout. Encourage the child in your life to take the first and hardest step: just start.

Let him know that you will help him along the way. Be the catalyst for your niece, nephew or cousin however you can – not just your own children. Sometimes well-meaning parents are too busy or unable to offer guidance and support because they don't know how. Here are four points to remember to develop young entrepreneurs:

1. As a parent, you see the vision
2. You help your child see the vision
3. Help them understand the vision
4. Help them determine how to implement the plan

While you will let your child have the final say and responsibility (within safe guidelines), help her think of ideas, solve problems and communicate those ideas in keeping with these four points. Remember, children are much more adaptive to new principles because they have no preconceived notions about things, which means they are more likely to embrace the optimism you assign them versus finding all the reasons why it can't work.

Raising a child is an opportunity to help build a brilliant mind so that creativity can blossom. Beyond the elementary years – in middle school, high school or college – students can start applying the lessons learned in areas of greater responsibility. Let's create smart, business savvy and financially astute young adults.

Granted, not every child is the same. We all know that children have different motivators, tolerance levels and personality characteristics. But the basic premise is to teach children to be higher level thinkers. We want right brained creativity to be built into a strong muscle, tempered by left-brained critical thinking to build a well-rounded pioneer.

If they believe there is power and merit in their thoughts and ideas, then you have created an influencer; one of the leaders of tomorrow. I'm sure you have heard people say, "I want to leave a legacy for my children." It should be, "I want to teach my children how to build a legacy." Or else, they might spend your legacy down to a bit of kindle for the fire, right out of the gate! Seriously, keep in mind that the biggest legacy is your child, and teaching him or her how to survive and thrive – that is a legacy in-and-of itself. Teach a man to fish… that is the smartest idea!
Don't be afraid of entering uncharted waters with your child. All ideas or products started with an idea or vision. It takes hope coupled with belief, which together can be called faith, as you will see this before it has happened. You see it in your mind before it manifests physically. Take care not to stifle a child's faith in his

or her abilities with your own unbelief that a child can create a viable income-producing idea or business. Think outside of the box, so that you can push them to do the same. Remember the first point: you need to see the vision, first.

In the example of the lemonade stand, you knew a lemonade stand was a good idea when your child asked; it's the sort of thing people like to contribute to, because they see the child's self-starting nature. You knew that it was a good illustration of a business with solid principles and also that your child would understand the business model, easily. The lesson: though life can make us cynical, don't discount the idea – give it the credence needed to see the vision.

Once you ask questions for more detail and you can see the vision, you can influence how your child develops his ideas. Let's not as parents be the cause of inhibitions and fear to develop, when at all possible. Don't suppress your child's vision with the negativity that you may have adopted over time. Remember get him to think like a business owner, and let him help you think like a child in your openness! Help him put thoughts into words and form a cohesive picture through the experience and knowledge that you have acquired. Remember the **C.L.E.V.E.R.** characteristics, to help see envision what you don't immediately see, yourself.

In some cases, it's going to be difficult for you to get your child to buy into the idea of a business. Think of child's interests (if she does not have her own idea) to suggest a business idea. Children do learn by example, but you can encourage a child to have a business, even if you don't have one, yourself. Don't let your negative thinking about the possibilities become an obstacle in the business.

In other cultures, it is actually quite common to develop young entrepreneurs, even despite relatively low socioeconomic class.

For example, a child in Peru is exposed to making shell necklaces in the family business. The child is witnessing the parents selecting materials for necklaces, determining the style, stringing the shells and selling them around town. It's their way of life.

I've been to other countries where children, siblings and parents alike participate in selling pottery and purses as well. In a somewhat similar model, say a medium-sized cattle feed business in Oklahoma, parents may own businesses which they hope are passed down to kids through the generations. Through this endowment-type process, and being in and around the business growing up, the child learns personality traits that lend to business ownership. Whether the child takes on the responsibility of the business is not always certain. However, they undoubtedly have that entrepreneurial blood and most times end up using those skills as their main income generator or even for a side-business to a different career.

We channel and foster the same character traits in kids. We use the **C.L.E.V.E.R.** characteristics to create good "soil" for our kids to be receptive and ready to become an entrepreneur. Now, let's go beyond the foundations to determine the qualities that help your child go the distance. What makes a successful entrepreneur?

- Positivity
- Critical thinking
- Leadership qualities
- Effective communication skills
- Good money management
- Forward-thinking nature
- Trendsetting

It's not unusual for kids to learn from their parents or in this case, even from their grandparents. We want to constantly plant seeds of greatness in our children. Many parents readily apply this principle in the lives of children as we help them develop self-control and kindness toward siblings, but typically not from the business frame-of-mind.

Sometimes this process happens naturally. A child that grows up around engineers (and might even have the same mechanically-inclined genes) might have tendency to study engineering. Seeing the example, though, is key. If a child spends his summer helping his father at the barber shop – sweeping floors, stacking magazines and seeing the business in operation – is more likely to be a business owner. In other cases, a child may not have grown up around business owners or have anyone they can glean from. My hope is this book will help to encourage the start of a business, given the foundational planning objectives and a framework of clear steps to develop entrepreneurs at any age. It doesn't matter if you don't have a vision to start with, or know what type of business you feel would be best, because God will always give you what you need and put resources in your path to reach the goals of business ownership and self-sufficiency!

Going through these steps in your mind, let yourself think of past comments your children have made. What ideas have they come up with around the dinner table in the past year that could have been reinforced and planted in your family? Keep in mind that you may help your child think of ideas, solve problems and communicate ideas while they are still taking ownership of them. Children are much more adaptive because they have an openness that will have been dampened to a degree by the time high school and college-age years roll around.

I am not claiming every child is the same; we all know that children have different motivators, tolerance levels and personality characteristics. However, the basic understanding is to meet them where they are and teach children to be creative, critical thinkers. If you have a child that is typically bursting with information, creating endless storylines with her favorite characters and looping everyone within arm's reach into the mix, the task at hand for parent or caregiver is more to channel that energy. Help her hone down her plentiful ideas to those with the most potential, using critical thinking questions. Develop ways to keep track of what was decided upon, should her mind drift and get off track to other ideas.

If your child is more reticent and typically takes quite some time observing before they jump in, promoting that creative energy is part of the game. Is he passionate about Teenage Mutant Ninja Turtles, producing countless caricatures of the four reptilians and assigning them to his friends and relatives? Seize an opportunity for him to grow and to give.

When he feels sad that Aunt Betty has fallen ill and he looks at you with disappointment that she won't be able to come to his birthday party, perhaps you suggest that he do something for Aunt Betty through his drawings. You might propose that raising money for a goodwill gesture of his choice can help her feel she is being thought of and part of the family. After a small venture into the money-making world by using the same creative skills for which your child has a passion, this stepping-stone might lead him to make his own suggestions in the future.

How to turn passion into profit? Going back to the lemonade stand example, many times it will be just this simple. Your child likes lemonade and since his friends like lemonade, he knew that there was a market (which is actual anecdotal data) so that is a good instinct; he knew that this is a group of people that would pay for the lemonade. By asking those questions to bring out the reasons behind his thinking, you are helping him see how he is already thinking like a business owner and he has been able to identify the principles of supply and demand. He is creating a product or service (supply) that others would buy and use (demand).

You can apply this to other businesses that adults own as well to drive the concept home. Everything is supply and demand: gasoline, roofing, housing, clothing, appliances… the list goes on and on. For each industry there is a potential micro business to be harnessed by a child who has a keen interest in the area.

Go get 'em. That interest is the seed for a product or service which will form a business. Here are the quick start steps so you can use these inklings as an open door to get your child's business going:

- Do an online search for what your child is interested in. In the information age, you can easily find a person, industry, job, product or profession that already exists… and then sell locally with better customer service or create a niche/improvement of the current version.
- Determine how much the item will cost to make, plus hours of labor to arrive at your price. Then start selling to your friends, family, neighbors and fellow students.
- Order business cards. Order them for free from online source like Vista Print. Or buy perforated cards at your local office supply store, then design and print them yourself.
- Make a sign with rates and go get 'em.

Once you realize this lemonade stand – or first entry into business – is really taking off, start making it official. You and your child might even be looking for a more lucrative, sustainable business or you want to scale what you have. These things will add credibility to the business, show that you have done your due diligence and further solidify your child's identity as an entrepreneur:

- Determine the business entity type by consulting an accountant on what makes sense for your circumstances
- Get a business license from your local municipality (either the county or city in which your business is located)

- Determine what licenses or certifications are needed for your industry
- Further define: who is your customer?
- Find out where will you buy the materials to make your product?
- Could you expand your product line, purchasing wholesale and selling with a markup?
- Register with the Secretary of State, if it is anything but a sole proprietorship
- Obtain a Tax ID number from the IRS
- If you are selling a product, you will need to collect sales tax, so create an account with the sales and use division in your state

After you are "officially" in business, you can then move onto problem solving, improving and expanding your business!

### • TIP•

Throughout childhood, give your child the impression that he must find his own way to go to school, and won't be living with you after graduating from college. Be clear that he can't rely on you for finding a job or a place to stay. The secret is you don't really mean this, but you are setting the expectation for him to be self-sufficient, and that will do much for his outlook. The actions of someone preparing to be independent are night-and-day, compared to youths that sleepily move into adulthood. It may be difficult, but you will be surprised! Your child will figure it out. I used to tell my teenage daughter that any drama involving her girlfriends was not my problem. If it didn't involve a threat to her life or abuse of any kind, I told her to work it out. The fights, disagreements and friends came and went. She was able to work it out every time every time I gave her the opportunity, with no further drama. Don't be a safety net, or you will forever be enabling your child to be less than her very best self.

## Chapter 6
## Implementing the Steps

> *"Faith without works is dead."*
> James 2:14

Intentions do not automatically translate to the accomplishment of goals. In a process of solidifying using critical thinking, goals must be worked into a plan of action. In the book, *Think and Grow Rich*, that was previously mentioned, included was the story of entrepreneur Barbara Gardner Proctor, who was raised by her grandmother. In short, the book explains how the young woman was born in a small town and her grandmother always told her to keep the faith, despite adversity.

Eventually, Barbara opened her own advertising agency. As difficult times surfaced in business, Barbara recalled her grandmother's words and how she showed her to stay the course in times of trouble. "In my hour of need, I found my greatest strength to be my grandmother's values," she remembered. "Keep the faith regardless of the appearance of things." Over and over, she recited those three words – keep the faith – until at each turning point, she overcame those obstacles. Her Chicago firm, Proctor & Gardner Advertising, was small but successful and made millions each year. In short, although Barbara's grandmother continuously told her to keep the faith, the real success was born out of the fact that she believed this through and through – and from that belief came the actions that produced her success.

Without the follow-through behind that faith, the words would have been lifeless. In essence, you need both.

So without delay, here are seven steps to take your child from vision to action. These are all adjectives: encourage, learn, teach, practice, realize, understand, and turn!

1. Encourage creative expression
2. Learn to seize opportunities
3. Teach children to recognize opportunities
4. Practice effective communication
5. Realize that failures are lessons to be learned
6. Understand lessons on saving, spending and giving
7. Turn passion into profit

**Step One: Encourage Creative Expression**

As shown from several angles now, belief is so important. Help your child see the vision. Allow him to be free to express his ideas without judging! When a child initially says, "Mommy, why don't we sell lemonade?" That is an opportunity to teach. That is your spark; that question is the chance to start creating a brilliant entrepreneurial mind. You might feel that in daily chores or in school subjects where he has no interest, your child is clumsy, forgetful or disorganized.

However, it doesn't mean he cannot be an effective business owner, yet. Your child has shown an interest in something. Use this high-interest area to build skills that trickle down to other areas as he realizes how competent he is, and how easy it is to get mundane things done when they are connected back to goals and purposes.

If she knows she can work for herself, turning her ideas into reality, then she can hire someone to help with organization. Don't miss this opportunity to connect with your child! Treat the initial question as a chance to harness a million-dollar idea and help her brainstorm and manifest great things! Think about supporters you may have had in your life, in your primary family or even with a teacher or coach. How confident do you think a child can become when you express an interest in what they do? When you pay attention and validate their ideas?

Continue to brainstorm with your child about his business or product idea, asking realistic questions. You asked questions about the lemonade stand such as, "To whom do we sell the lemonade?" and "What are the things needed to make the lemonade?" You asked, "How much do the supplies to make this cost?"

Develop an atmosphere where he expects these questions and knows that he can trust you to help. So in this way, your child expects that if he wants to do something, he will need to become a critical thinker and work out these issues out under your guidance. Over time he might even be able to predict what type of questions he needs to ask and information he needs in order to put the puzzle pieces together for a new business. As you question him, he is also learning how to handle objections from a trusted source and communicate the explanation about the "who-what-when-where and whys" with confidence. The process of the question and answer introspection combines the right-side creativity with the left-side critical thinking. Even better, because young children are impressionable, you can convince them they can do anything. If you believe it, he will believe it, too!

Before we continue to discuss developing your child's brilliant entrepreneurial mind, we must deal with the questionable mindset of well-meaning adults that you will no doubt encounter (or perhaps this person is you!). Be reminded that all ideas or products started with an idea or vision, even Ford Motor Company and other business giants. The vision is called having faith because you are seeing it before it has happened.

You must see it in your mind before it manifests in the physical, and if you are not used to this concept, it can seem like a pipe dream. Literally every company had to start small with good business principles, and either keep reinvesting profits to grow bit-by-bit, or prove their idea and business-management savvy to investors.

Don't be fooled by the fear that starting small will produce nothing of meaningful value; by doing this, you can stifle a child's creative ability and squelch a potentially income-producing idea or business. Instead, think outside of the box; push them! Remember the first point: as the mature adult and leader, you need to see the vision first. In the example of the lemonade stand, you knew that one stand was able to produce at least a measured amount of profit and would teach needed principles when you received the query.

You must be willing to take it slow at your child's pace, and witness some hard work being done as the gears start turning in your her brain, as the basic lessons are learned. Don't discount the idea or vision due to doubts about the growing pains that will occur during this period. Start at square one, and this will lead to bigger and better things. Child-sized bites. Don't figure it out for them; let them experience the discomfort of this learning period – simply back it up with your encouragement. You will always be there if they fall. Once you see the vision, though, you can influence how your child sees it by the nature of your attitude.

Be aware of your own responses to issues that come up. Will you simply ask with a positive attitude how we can get around the issue? Or would your expressions or attitude about an obstacle betray your confidence in your child? Inspect your own attitudes and those of others around you as you begin this process, so that you can be sure to respond affirmatively when issues come up. You don't want to be the impetus for inhibitions and fear to develop. If you feel that you have adopted negativity over time, take time to further study how businesses have started and matured so that you can be ready!

I simply know you don't want a starving artist as a grown adult child who you must continue to support, or have kids that are not self-sufficient through encouraging crazy entrepreneurial ideas, but turn this fear upside down! This process is the exact way to encourage her to be self-sufficient.

What are we doing by asking, "Why do you want to start a lemonade stand, and who is your customer?" We are creating a path to entrepreneurship, but your child is paving the way with her own answers. You are helping her see the vision through knowing the right questions to ask, having already created a general picture in your mind.

However, you don't answer the questions for him. How else might you help your child see the vision? Glad you asked! In the process we have been studying, you ask your child questions not just about "what" the plan is, but also "why" he likes this particular idea and "how" he plans to implement it. You might ask your child to draw out his plans. This is called mind-mapping. Some learners are auditory (we talk it out and walk someone through each of our thoughts) and some are visual (draw it out; make flow charts, draw the design of the actual lemonade stand, draw the happy faces of the customers to truly see the goal). In our fast-paced society and as influencers recognize differing learning styles, notice how infographics are growing with popularity. You can paint a picture on paper to further clarify the goals of the business.

As a child gets older, keep this same model. Don't be moved by outside detractors that say that your child's idea won't work. And let her see your position in response to any unfounded criticism, as well. An older child may have an idea, but a couple handfuls of doubts to go along with it. She might mention this idea in a passive way, even stating in the first sentence, "I know it would never actually work, but…." Again, go back to the first point, as this is your chance to see the vision first in this potentially million dollar idea, and help her see the merit behind it, so she catches the vision, too. Don't let her say "no" to herself, before their potential customer actually says "no." Adopt an attitude to try it! This is a common business principle, Let them say their own 'no's. Keep reading for more help in with dealing with older children, as well!

### • TIP •

Learn to listen more and talk less even with kids. It's the reason we have one mouth and two ears…

**Step Two: Learn to Seize Opportunities**
After you and your child recognize an opportunity, help him seize it. Children learn by example, and seeing you take advantage of an opportunity when it presents itself with a growth mindset will create an atmosphere of confidence.

Growth mindset, a concept formed by Stanford University psychologist Carol Dweck, describes the state when people believe that their most basic abilities can be developed through dedication and hard work. By contrast, with a fixed mindset, people believe the basic qualities they possess are most important for success, like intelligence or talent, are simply fixed traits. You either have it or you don't, with this mindset. Some people will view the hard work associated with taking advantage of opportunities as such a drawback that they will not engage; the risk seems too great.

Teach your children that your invested effort multiplies! Many don't know that they can "do hard things" and how rewarding it is, many times yielding results that are tenfold compared to the resources invested. This is good for kids to see – let them see you tackle challenges. Kids need to see role models taking on difficult tasks because they know hard work pays off. And, there are less role models for them to learn from as society in the information age becomes increasingly digitized; each member of the family has become more detached and isolated. Sense of community has been drained.

The spirit of collaboration has been lost as communities grow out and apart from each other. We are losing the village mentality in most cultures. In the past, businesses were built on the support and work of all the family members. Everyone in the family had a vested interest. Societies have gotten away from this model. So, most kids don't see families working together, or communities working together, for that matter. All this makes it less likely for kids to come up with an idea to share to their circle of family and friends. Instead, conversation is giving way to solitary activity as less and less is expected of kids, and their gaming pursuits fill up their schedules. Less of their thoughts are actually put into words. And sharing with another is psychologically an important step! Do everything you can to increase the interconnectedness; for a child to see a good idea blossom into a fruit-producing tree is so impactful. He can learn to work with others in implementing business ideas.

Another benefit to bringing back the lost art of collaboration is leaning on the strength of others. Most businesses fail because the owner wears too many hats. After a few trays of bread get burnt because the same individual is busy trying to do a little inventory or handle customers, small business owners realize that they can't do everything effectively in a silo. When you learn to delegate work and change how you view the tasks that need to be completed, you are able to both recognize your own strengths and learn where others are stronger or weaker in the same areas.

Ever wonder why kids groan when they are given group projects in school? These are growing pains. It almost hurts us sometimes to give up part of our projects, because we are giving up control. A young age is a great time teach collaboration, when the brain is more malleable. She will be able to rely on the strength of someone else and they will rely on her skills. Think of what a confidence-builder that will be as she becomes part of an effective team!

Due to the pervasive need for your child to eventually work with others to get large scale projects completed, he will be much more successful in business if these skills are learned early. The advice given to new salespeople is to shadow and tag-team a strong salesperson in the industry. In those early days, it is essential to find a role model. Rather than reinventing the wheel, success comes much more easily when using a tried-and-true path.

Unfortunately, some feel that it means they do not have enough innate talent if they don't carve their own path. If your child seems to feel this way, the best thing to emphasize is hard work. Not everyone is willing to be diligent, overcome obstacles and do the menial tasks required in the early years of business. Let him know there is no shame in following someone else's model.

The blockbuster movie The Pursuit of Happyness depicted the real life struggle of Chris Gardner. One day, homeless Gardner saw a man driving a very expensive sports car. He asked what the man did for a living, and he stated that he was a stockbroker. Gardner saw and felt the proof of that man's success, seeing the reality that he wanted for himself and his child in that car. Gardner saw a path out of homelessness.

He was in sales, but did not know all that the new position would entail. However, he knew he had a choice to make. Gardner interned to learn the business, making a wage that was not enough to pay expenses or put a roof over his son's head. But he had grit and determination, and he had set his mind when he was five years old that his children would see a good example. He emulated the successful brokers until he became successful himself, despite not having a good start in life. In a way, he had to put his ego aside in order to focus on his goal, one that would benefit those around him.

Seizing the opportunity pays off. Two sisters, ages nine and ten, who had been raised up learning about their mother's business started their own enterprise, and were featured in the Atlanta Business Chronicle. Their mother had been taught the same enterprising values from her parents, and she wanted to pass the torch on to her kids. I was so excited that the mother taught her daughters to seize opportunities and had such faith in the principles she was taught. Now in their teens, online sales for their business have exceeded $70,000 and they have grown the company from having three employees to 25!

At the time of the article, they had also just secured a deal to sell in a major retail outlet. When you find someone that is doing what you would like to do or whom you can emulate, it's important to reach out. You never know where that connection can take you. How beautiful that we have other parents out there giving merit to the idea of teaching children how to be business owners.

• TIP •

This is about teaching your child to seize the opportunity when he finds an interest, so be careful not to force your own interests on him!

**Step Three: Teach Children to Recognize Opportunities**
When your child comes up with an idea, help extend it so the child can see the vision. We want this type of enterprising mind to be passed on so that they, too, will have vision, passion and ideas that should be harnessed and expressed. We should not automatically be funneling our children down the path of what is commonly thought to be secured income by raising lawyers, doctors or engineers. Not to be misunderstood, higher education is extremely valuable, but we need to help students become

problem solvers. Show them not just "what to think" as many times the educational system is trying to do, but how to think better.

Many kids today are thought of as being entitled, complaining when things are not convenient or not handed to them on a silver platter. Developing those problem-solving skills as a basic outlook on life helps students to be a part of a solution rather than being part of the peanut gallery. This type of outlook will be used over and over again as a business owner.

A creative thinker focuses on how to get the job done, and done more effectively. You take the child's passion and fire it in the oven with critical thinking, planning and executional skills and it becomes a breeding ground. She will be able to develop something greater than the sum of its parts. A brilliant business mind can come from a student that excels or does not excel academically. This can be a child that's considered different – Einstein was! If she learns differently, she has the ability to think differently, and that is more than acceptable. That creative expression is an opportunity for you and your child. Thinking outside of the box isn't normal, either. So embrace these qualities in your child and let them flourish.

In short, don't dismiss a child's idea – it's possible that it might not seem like much at first, but there is a reason he is telling you. Find out the reason with probing questions! Multi-million dollar Post-it® Notes started as a flopped trial at a new super glue. The glue used for these handy notes just wasn't sticky enough. But the inventor persisted and championed his new glue for years within the 3M company as a solution to a problem that many would appreciate, and now the notes are a household item.

Great inventions are created from an idea and at the very least, when you treat it like a possible winner, a child begins to feel empowered by his idea. It starts with a vision, then action follows to bring the plan to fruition. If you continuously to denounce his ideas at first mention, you will begin to smother any future thoughts and opinions.

• TIP •

Notice and encourage your child's natural abilities and promote their implementation in her business.

**Step Four: Practice Effective Communication**
Teach children to assert themselves and clearly explain their ideas and thoughts. With the lemonade stand, we started with a child that had an idea for selling the sweet treat, and ended up being able to thoughtfully explain who will purchase the lemonade, if the business idea makes sense financially and why someone would want to purchase lemonade from the stand. This tiny crash course has already developed a new child who has a reason to communicate something persuasively to you, all because you encouraged an idea to form into a vision.

You are also helping your child have confidence in his vision, as in the case of needing to present to you when they want a new toy or latest gadget. By not over-reaching to provide something when it is not yet earned, you are stating, "I trust that you can come up with the reasons for your needs and desires." By not giving the answer or vigorous head nods right away, you are telling your child, "You can have confidence in the words you have spoken. You may or you may not receive this item, but you have made your case and you can know that you have done a good job."

Over time, he will learn to be decisive, confident and more persuasive in his techniques and you will see this in his interaction with others. If he receives a "B" on a paper that was excellent compared to his peers, don't be surprised if you notice that he petitions the teacher for an "A" grade! The skills that are taught through business communication will adjust his every step through life.

I worked for Waffle House® in my early career. It was fascinating that the owner of several hundred restaurants could review the profit and loss statements for the respective stores, at a glance he would know if the expenses were high and needed to be adjusted, or whether the store was doing an exceptional sales volume.

He knew the approximate number of eggs and chicken breasts that were needed in order to accommodate a certain number of customers. Once that formula was down, he could apply it to any location based on the volume of the store. In short, if the numbers were off, he knew it was theft, carelessness or waste. Based on having this skill, he knew the numbers when he approached a particular store and was able to clearly communicate to managers how to handle the problem at hand. Being an effective communicator is essential in business. An idea is an amorphous quantity and needs to be defined. Determining who will buy and demonstrating the product to those potential customers is essential. This is the start of the communication process – right at the beginning! Next, the entrepreneur must request funding from various sources, deal with employees and work with others on issues that arise to solve problems and stay competitive. It all revolves around the use of effective communication.

Negotiating and communication skills go hand-in-hand. There are a wealth of books available to build negotiating skills. Many times, people view negotiating as being difficult or combative. So, if you can master the art of negotiation, you are already much further along than most. The best way to view negotiating is merely a conversation to get to a consensus about a particular product or service. Just because you want to negotiate a position does not mean you must haggle or become difficult.

It also does not equate to one party taking advantage of the other. I have always found myself in positions in my career where I have been able to find a solution for all parties, and that is highly satisfying. I get to work with others toward a common goal. We don't want to fall into the common "one-up, one-down" philosophy that I will win if the other party loses. In business done right, there are ways for all parties to walk away pleased. Example: your child has a business selling decorative pencils to classmates. Johnny wants to buy in bulk – five pencils at a time, because he tends to lose some to his siblings. So, he wants a better price for all five together, which is acceptable because your child gets to move more volume. She might take a small cut in margin but ends up with more sales at the end of the day. Both parties are happy.

At a recent networking breakfast, the topic was the art of negotiation. He gave the example of business in real estate: you are working for the common goal of selling the house for the seller and finding a house for the buyer. This is good for everyone and he said sales should really be simplified. You are merely pairing people and services, and it produces a win-win situation – and is how all business should be. We overthink the process. Whether a product or service, you are putting the two together. How simple is that to teach a child?

This reminds me of a story as told by entrepreneur and philanthropist Mark Cuban. Cuban owns the NBA Dallas Mavericks and several entertainment companies. But he explained that these entrepreneurial endeavors began with simple lessons he learned as a child. When Mark asked his dad for a pair of expensive sneakers, his dad responded that the shoes on his feet looked like they're working pretty well. He went on to state, "If you want a new pair of sneakers, you need a job and you can go buy them." Cuban had no clue where he could get a job as a 12-year-old.

His dad's friend chimed in and suggested that Mark sell garbage bags. He further explained the idea to Cuban. The cost for 100 bags is $3 and he could make an additional $3 per box, parsing out portions of the box to his customers. He sold the bags door to door. Cuban said he practiced his pitch just so: "Hi, does your family use garbage bags?" Who could say no, that they don't use garbage bags… and especially to a kid?

That was his first lesson in business; buy the bulk product for less, sell individually for more. Going door to door helped him deal with objections. He would practice his response: "Of course you use garbage bags, and I bet you pay more than six cents apiece." He was able to save enough to buy the sneakers, and more. He used the same simple premise for other businesses, and the rest was history.

It's a simple premise; pair the product to the person and ask for the business. There's no better way to learn negotiation than with practice. If you can teach your child how to negotiate, she will be better served in any setting.

• TIP •

When your child wants something, like a toy, he must give three valid reasons why he should have the item. This is considered your child's proposal.

**Step Five: Realize that Failures are Lessons to Be Learned**
It is proper to fail in sales and in business. We must receive no many times before we can get to the yes. This is in the right order because we also know that asking for business means the word no will be heard more than yes. Getting the feedback can also help us to know the market. What are people willing to buy, and at what price? Do we have enough value to tip the scale in our favor? The advantage for young entrepreneurs is that kids haven't experienced enough disappointment yet to expect it. Children naturally have that faith. After all, they play make-believe all the time. They may have an imaginary friend who you can't see,

but who is very real in his mind. It's important not to stifle his endless imagination. He has no reason to believe that he cannot accomplish a goal! He doesn't have bills, responsibilities, negative influences or other people telling him that he can't accomplish his goals.

As he grows older and develops more reason, your job is still to encourage him; reframe what it means when he didn't get the sale. This is a natural part of the process – this is what is supposed to happen. So, when he does hear the word no, he isn't fazed, broken, wounded, distraught or disappointed. It's either, 'How can I make the presentation or product better?' or on to the next opportunity. The lesson to learn is to move beyond the word no – do not stop right as you are about to get to the good stuff! What if the idea does not take off, or the business isn't successful? Well, at young age, success is subjective.

Did she learn something from it; did she have fun executing the process? The life lesson for the child is in creating and developing a business, whether it continues or not.

Realize that failure is a lesson to be learned. Helping a child to see the vision means seeing past the challenges that are inevitably presented, learning lessons on failure, and moving past these to solve issues that arise. The best way for them to learn these lessons is while they have a safety net – you. Zig Ziglar said, "Failure is an event, not a person." Business magnate Henry Ford said, "Failure is the opportunity to begin again more intelligently." Take these truisms to heart. The outlook these folks had on failure is part of the reason why they were able to gain success. If the idea or business did not work, it's time for another life lesson. Begin again, better.

When you begin anew, take stock of how things could've gone differently. How can your child learn from the experience? What if you didn't sell any lemonade? Your child has the opportunity to question why lemonade isn't selling. Not from a place of sadness, but as a scientist would study a phenomenon and create a hypothesis. Could the lemonade be too tart or too sweet? Then, what could be done to remedy this issue? The business owner may need to have taste testers to get it just right. Start with a great product or service. Now, he is becoming a problem solver to make the product better – and collaborating with others to gain a consensus.

This methodology can be practiced even before he becomes a business owner by gaining experience in internships or volunteering. More importantly, when you are speaking with your child and trying to walk her through examining what could have gone differently, notice your own feelings about the failed attempt. Do you feel down on yourself or your child for the way it went? What is your tone when speaking to her about the lesson? Are you rubbing her back and uttering consoling phrases, "So sorry that it didn't work out. It's okay, it's okay." Avoid this! Know that children are resilient.

By doing this, you are teaching her that what she did in the pioneering attempt is actually a sad thing, when it is actually so positive that she tried! Treat her as the strong person she is. Know that she can handle this. If she seems down, don't sway in your approach. Just keep asking, "So what do you think could have made it go better?"

Emphasize that your child should not have feelings of regret and doubt in decisions she made if things didn't go as planned. Another lesson on failure is, don't let the four-letter word creep in: fear. Inspirational actor Will Smith has famously said, "Fear is not real. The only place that fear can exist is in our thoughts of the future. It is a product of our imagination, causing us to fear things that do not at present and may not ever exist."

In other words, when you want to succeed, fear is not an option. It sounds simple… but removing this "bad word" from your vocabulary and thought processes can be difficult to implement. Ironically, we are not born with fear. It's the reason babies can swim at birth; it is instinctive. Fear of the water is something that is developed! Having disappointing past experiences with less-than-desirable outcomes is how fear develops. It is possible that your child might bring up some fears about starting anew. However, it is how a child responds to fear that is the important part. By working through fear to see the light at the end of the tunnel, new pathways can be formed in the brain.

So next time another obstacle is encountered, it will seem like just that. An obstacle. Something to get over and beyond or to find a way around. Help your child redirect the energy from fear towards the desired goal during that period. Fear is simply misdirected apprehension about moving forward, so focusing on the fear is not helpful.

Helping a child to see the vision means receiving lessons on failure, too. As stated, failure is a lesson best learned while they have a safety net so that you can help them process what is happening. If the idea or business did not work, it's time for another life lesson. Perhaps chart out the "who-what-when-where-why" on paper. List where you started: to whom did you aim to sell the lemonade; what types of lemonade and what recipe; what time of day did you sell it; at what locations did you set up shop and why did you choose to sell it in the first place?

Now, you have a model from which you can determine what should remain the same and what could be different. Perhaps the recipe was exceptional, but the street corner where the stand was stationed did not get a lot of foot traffic. Or perhaps the lemonade was priced for adults during the summer when the kids are out of school riding bikes around the neighborhood. Whatever changes are to be made, emphasize that your child should not have feelings of regret or doubt about decisions they chose, if it did not go completely as planned.

Steve Harvey made it simple when he said, "Failure is a valuable learned experience. It teaches you what not to do." It's especially interesting for the young, because the world is more forgiving as a child. You should learn when you fail.

• TIP •

When a disappointment occurs, ask your child how they are feeling, and listen, then reinforce that disappointment does not define them as a person.

**Step Six: Understand Lessons on Saving, Spending and Giving**
Congratulations, your child now has a mechanism to make money! But what would a lesson in entrepreneurship be without showing your child what to do with money once he has it? Should he spend it all on the latest sports jersey he has been eyeing? Share it with friends and become their one stop shop for jolly ranchers and lemon drops on the school bus? You can see how a great lesson might turn sour, fast, under these conditions.

As an adult, he might have one short-lived business success after another, but not being able to manage money and put it to good use will cut the legs off of any operation. Remember Kanye West's 2016 Twitter pleas to the Facebook and Google founders to loan him $1 billion? In the previous three years, he reportedly took in $72 million in revenue from albums and concerts. However, he ended up in $53 million in debt by the end of that time from ventures in the fashion industry, and wanted bailouts from others so that he could continue his creative endeavors.

True, it's possible that the rapper could have brought beautiful things to the world with that bailout money. But that is an extremely unhealthy cycle for him to be in, which does not help him to be grounded, stable or independent. Lessons on spending, saving and giving are for all ages. And it is an important part of any business. Depending on how your child thinks and processes information, you will want to use one of the below methods. You can try them at different times and switch based on the response it produces.

Developing money-mindedness. Each method begins with a bank account. Allow the child to go to the bank, complete a deposit slip, walk to the counter and make their own deposit. Teach your child to double-check the amount before walking away. You want to create a good experience around going to the bank, giving him a feeling of accomplishment.

Adding to this by teaching the value of money, a great option is to take your child to the grocery store. Managing a weekly grocery budget, evaluating whether certain items really need to be purchased and comparing the cost per unit on the price stickers is a way to learn what things cost and understand the concept of money. At the same time, you will be empowering your child by giving her small areas of decision-making. Although it takes more time to teach these concepts to children and have them go through the practice, it helps her understand that money is a real thing; it is not infinite.

Also in conjunction with a bank account, you may use a chore chart that will provide a pathway to money for extra chores in the household to be completed that are above-and-beyond what she would normally do. If she shows industriousness in this area, diligently working on them in an independent fashion, she can earn some allowance.

Complete an agreement in writing, listing the chores to be done every week and the respective compensation for each. The agreement should indicate when chores will be complete. For example, by Saturday at 3 p.m., all chores for the week must be completed. There is a reasonable amount assigned to each chore (not too much, or it will distort the value of money). At the end of the week, she is paid based on which chores were completed within the time period. Keep in mind that if the chores are considered late, they are still required and must be done – but no compensation is gained, because they were not completed by the day and time on the agreement. You and your child should sign and date the agreement.

For parents that don't like the idea of allowance or giving chores, here's another suggestion. Instead, the child must determine what needs to be done around the house to create his own allowance. For example: clean the garage, basement or attic. The child should make their request known, set the price and negotiate the rate of pay explaining how he came up with the proposed rate.

This allows him to show more leadership in thinking outside of the box, not simply fulfilling a requirement, which could be more attractive. It requires both critical and creative thinking. In this way, he is the impetus for his own change; not simply being satisfied with what is given. He also learns that hard work, accomplishing a goal and negotiating the rate under his own gumption has a reward. And some children may be more motivated to follow through because they have chosen the list of chores and specifics.

For kids that have a job or are not motivated by money, you could implement reverse-commission. In other words, your child will pay you a commission as a penalty for chores that have not been completed. Have a list of the completed chores each week. If the chores are not completed by the end of the week, your child has to pay you a fee. In this case as well, the chores still need to be completed, but there is a penalty for not doing them in a timely fashion.

Another idea for kids with income is to assign a bill for the child to pay each month. Collect the money religiously, not allowing them to skip a payment. Without the child knowing, use the money for their savings or an investment for them. After they have grown, they can use it toward the future purchase of a home, investment property, car or even a business.

The premise of spending, saving, and giving can be demonstrated by talking through the lemonade stand example. Your child must determine how much sugar, lemons and lemonade mix is needed to make a pitcher of lemonade. And how many cups of lemonade can one pitcher can produce. Thus, they have figured gross profit. The cost of the sugar, lemons and lemonade mix is calculated. The gross profit minus the expenses equals net profit; this is how much money will be left over after expenses.

So now that we have defined net profit, we should consider how much should be reinvested into the business. After all, once you have a business that can generate a profit, it is crucial to then grow the business to achieve true success. That's the savings parallel for children receiving money – they would bank that portion when they are receiving these money lessons from you, even if they are not reinvesting at the time. Secondly, how much will you spend on other expenses to expand or add another lemonade stand or salaries?

That's the spending parallel to the other income your child may receive. You can see how an illustrative example (owning a business) will provide this example so naturally. Thirdly, businesses do give back to the community in many ways with scholarships, sponsorships and donations. That's the giving – buying little brother a ticket to the science museum he has been wanting to visit as a birthday present, for example.

Lessons on spending, saving and giving are for all ages and it's an important part of any business. Because children are created with different learning styles, provided here are different methods. Try them at different times to see how they respond. Regardless of the method chosen, start with the bank account and allow your child to have ownership over that! Money earned will be deposited with pride.

• TIP •

As your child gets older, use the grocery store as your training ground by looking at products and prices to determine what deal is best.

**Step Seven: Turn Passion into Profit**
Turn passion into profit. Do you remember the commercial with the guy who had the monotonous task of making the donuts every morning? How miserable it can be to go to a job that you hate, showing up at 8 a.m. every morning because you have to, not because you want to be there? This is the time to teach children to find what they love. In other words, take your child's interest and determine a way to make it a viable business. Help your child understand the plan.

This feeds into the idea of helping your child see the vision in the idea they have produced and having unwavering belief. Your presence as a support for your child's vision is essential. Your skills in listening to and helping him to develop his idea will be the key factor in his early success. In 1961, John F. Kennedy announced that he wanted to send an American to the moon by the end of the decade. The announcement made before a joint session of congress – and before the country at large – did a lot to contribute to the fulfillment of that goal. Stating your goals out loud to others makes them much more likely to come to fruition.

Just over 40 years after Apollo 11 put the first man on the moon, another pioneer with a huge vision for making waves in outer space accomplished something no other private company has done. Elon Musk's SpaceX was the first private company to launch, orbit and bring a spacecraft back down to earth successfully in 2010. Musk has a "why" attached to this feat which occurred just eight years after the company's launch. Other companies Musk founded include electric car manufacturer Tesla, Inc. and a solar energy company SolarCity. Importantly, several of these companies including SpaceX and Tesla have a common goal to change the nature of how we live life. Musk wants to reduce carbon emissions and pave the way for humanity to live sustainably on Mars to reduce the possibility of extinction. How's that for a mission!

It doesn't matter if your child's mission is a bit smaller – such as brightening the day of Ms. Hendricks down the street who doesn't get a lot of visitors. It's equally justified for your child to have big dreams of being the innovator to make the hovercrafts of Back to the Future a reality for the common consumer. What is important is to identify those areas of interest, develop them and find out what is behind them. When you plant those seeds – more interests, ideas and passions will spring out of them. If your child does like the concept of engineering and saw a summer science camp opportunity that she wanted to work toward, can you imagine what great ideas she might produce after visiting this camp? We need to pick up on those notes of interest and help the child run with them.

Simon Sinek, author of Start With Why, says there is a pattern to the great innovative giants in our economy. For example, he references Apple, Inc. and poses the question: why is Apple so innovative year after year, when they have access to all the same talent, consultants and feedback from consumers on what they desire?

Or what is the reason that the Wright brothers achieved powered flight in 1903, when there were undoubtedly others working on the same idea who were more qualified and had more funding? Sinek postulates that the reason why some organizations are able to inspire and others are not is because instead of starting with the what, or even the more philosophical how, they started with why. He says that most all employees are able to communicate what the company does (the what).

Some of them might even be able to communicate the how, meaning the unique value proposition of the company or perhaps their proprietary process. But even fewer know why. For the owner of a company, to know your why, one must ask questions such as the following more foundational queries. What is your purpose? What is your cause, belief – what makes you get out of bed in the morning? He further states that people don't buy what you do, they buy why you do it. If you have connected with something that you believe in, you can inspire the sale. You can achieve more.

When a child states that he wants to go to the moon, it is crucial that we don't extinguish his passion. He may, or he may not. But by allowing him to explore these passions and find out what he can do today that will relate to his goal, even if in a very small way (could he create videos on ad-serving platforms inspiring other young thinkers to go for their dreams, too?) he will get closer and closer to his why. His dreams might take twists and turns, and one dream may very well lead to another. But in their early imaginative states, the potential to practice building those muscles – which both form identity and tell him what he is about – is endless. In other words, make sure to encourage his exploration of why he wants to pursue the things that he brings up, even casually in conversation.

• TIP •

Be your child's 401K when it comes to earnings for material possessions or experiences. When they see something they want, ask what money they have for this item, and let them know you will match them dollar-for-dollar with your money. Works every time to help your child know if it is something they really want.

## Chapter 7
## Create a Business Plan

> *"Failing to plan is planning to fail."*
> Alan Lakein

Putting pen to paper will help clarify the plan of action in developing the new business. The plan does not have to be elaborate but must have some crucial components. The business plan should follow the S.M.A.R.T. goals philosophy. So, the plan for the business will be Specific, Measurable, Attainable, Relevant and Time Sensitive!

A business plan will make your child answer pertinent questions for any business, which are the same questions we reviewed in the lemonade stand example. Why do I want to sell lemonade? How much will I charge? Who will buy it? How much can I make? How can I grow the business?

These fundamentals will in time sprout growth in the form of new questions about development and expansion, especially after the initial trials. Should we offer frozen lemonade? How will it stay frozen? Does the new product require additional equipment, and if so – what is the cost of the equipment? Perhaps your child decides to expand by placing lemonade stands in more than one location. Wow, now she is thinking like a true entrepreneur!

The business plan forces you to think about the steps and long-term goals. There are many business plan guides available for study. Here is a basic abbreviated version.

nswer the following questions in your business plan:

- The mission statement or goal of the business (start with your why!)
- Who is your customer?
- What are the materials needed to start?
- List examples of who has successfully done what you are attempting to accomplish.
- Do you have competition? Who?
- How will you market your business?
- How will you grow the business or what are the continued plans to keep selling your product or service?
- Are your plans to expand your business, or sell it? The exit strategy is the capstone to the business plan.

Writing out answers to the above questions in paragraph form will help you develop a clear path to reach your goals. This describes the basics of what, how and why you will develop this business. For this reason, you should never enter into a business relationship with anyone without completing a business plan. You can then see how your ideals for the business and your partner's may be similar or different. You might find even a good friend or family member with whom you have shared many years may have different business expectations than yours. It is better to address those concerns before entering into the business relationship and it becomes convoluted.

 Implement the seven steps as in Chapter 6, realizing that as parents we must see the vision, help our children to see the vision, help them understand the vision and help them work the plan.  When you operate using these habits, you are creating a legacy by developing a brilliant entrepreneurial mind in our greatest assets: our children. (And you will keep those adult children couch potatoes at bay!) It's important to teach and practice the steps provided to result in self-sufficient, empowered and business-savvy children!

I had to follow my own advice by setting S.M.A.R.T. goals to complete this book. At the start of any project, it may seem too great to accomplish. After all, at the time of writing the book, I was working full time, growing another business with the family and of course had kids to raise. I had an epiphany as I was reading Superpower by Ford Saeks. It's about using technology as a time-saver, rather than a time-waster.

The book mentioned an app that helps with time management, and it was like the light bulb came on. I decided to turn my "lemons into lemonade" with the book. I began using a talk-to-text app to dictate each chapter. I was reminded that regardless of the circumstances, to stay the course one must be resilient! In those moments, you realize you can always learn and evolve into something better than you were before. Moving onward toward completion of the book was now the goal. No matter the circumstances, you can alter your outcome with hard work, resilience and faith. We'll talk more about faith later in the book.

To make my goal timely, I decided to set a completion date. Setting the parameters forced me to get closer to the goal. I used my otherwise fruitless time sitting in traffic to record the book with talk-to-text. I later converted the text to an MS Word document and began the writing process. The way in which the goals are achieved is relative to your current position. The point is to set measurable goals and take steps to achieve them. Teach your children to use the same approach. It can be applied in many areas, personal and professional, throughout life.

### • TIP •

Have your child think of an example of something they wanted and name the actions they did to get the item or accomplish the goal. We are doing a little example of cause and effect to help your child understand that the cause or intentionality brings about a result.

## Chapter 8
## Are Entrepreneurs Born or Bred?

> *"Courage is the most important of all the virtues because without courage, you can't practice any other virtue consistently."*
> Maya Angelou

Is entrepreneurship taught or is it instinctive? You are going to be very surprised by my response. We can find the answers through many real-life scenarios. It is not the popular opinion, especially to parents of young children, that many entrepreneurial traits are in-born, but many times this is certainly the case. This is not to say that largely genetic traits cannot be developed, still, just that there are some things that will come easier and some with more effort. However, as parents we of course encourage many traits to form over childhood and do not leave everything to nature.

Take confidence, for one. Certainly, one of the points of this book is that we can develop traits that are currently in their infancy and create a more balanced individual who is better prepared to face the world as an adult. However, twin studies have shown that much of confidence is genetic.

Researchers compared identical twins with fraternal twins (with fraternal twins sharing only the environment, and identical twins in the same household sharing both genes and environment). When children rated their school performance in comprehensive testing, the genes were a more likely predictor of their confidence and also their success in school, when researchers looked at the outcomes.

Confidence comes up again and again as a trusted friend in many of our described entrepreneurial characteristics to be developed. Determination can be backed by confidence; creative vision backed by hopeful confidence; a spirit of excellence which gives way to the energy needed to perform well – also backed by the confidence (along with it, a "can-do" attitude that the child can get the job done.)

Research self-confidence online and you will clearly find a wealth of ways to improve it. You can practice mindfulness, set goals, break things down into smaller tasks to practice getting them done, take measured risks and stand up for yourself. One of the best ways to encapsulate all of these things, and also find ways to improve another largely innate trait – passion – is to use the vehicle of entrepreneurship for that little (or not-so-little) person in your life. Thus, the aim of this book!

As parents, we want the best for our children. To speak of the anxious game parents play to determine how many activities would-you-should-you involve your child in, I've been there. Halfway hoping the activity betters the child; halfway hoping the child conquers the activity. I put my kids in every activity they were remotely interested in. They were able to try out different sports, instruments, dabble in science, get creative in arts, espouse the virtues of theatre and the list goes on. In the end, the child's intrinsic abilities naturally rise to the top, and you spring into action by feeding that talent.

It's the same in recognizing entrepreneurial characteristics; as we've discussed, some core characteristics have a quite an in-born foundation. Now, to provide an opportunity for your child to be well-rounded, there are also some that can be modeled and learned through the hands-on experience. Your child might naturally stand up for what she wants (never thought you would be thankful that they spaghetti landed on the floor when she was a toddler, did you?!), but how to use assertiveness correctly in effective communication is learned. Your child may have been born with a "join the cause" and forge ahead type of attitude, or may need to observe for some time before becoming comfortable. Perhaps he has always joined you in sweeping the floor and spraying down the mirror from a wee 18 months old. But that willingness to do hard work can be seasoned with proven success so the hard work plus the "wins" experienced create grit that will bring much success.

Child psychologists name many in-born factors that make up temperament, which describe how even an infant will interact with her world. The basis of emotional intensity, likelihood of overwhelm with sensory experiences, activity level, adaptability and persistence are credited to be present at birth.

Your job as a parent is to provide exposure to practical lessons (many times in the form of organized activities nowadays) and to see what resonates with your child. In this way, you will help him to be the very best that he can be by expanding his positive traits and allowing new ones to blossom through experiential lesssons. When the brain connections are "pruned" in the early 20s, whatever has not been used and developed tends to wither and die off. However, no matter what the parent magazines, books and therapists say, you cannot "make a child good at something." Parents are in denial, or more to the point, living vicariously through their kids, by insisting a child continue to participate in something they don't like and aren't good at it. It's unhealthy and isn't in the spirit of helping the child find out where his natural propensities lie.

Not to be misunderstood; a child should not quit simply because a task is difficult – especially not in the middle of a season. It's also true that a child doesn't know what she doesn't know, so this is a good reason to provide repeated encouragement to keep trying. Introduce the activity, have the her put forth her best effort. If she is really good at it, then continue to feed the craft, support and in some cases compel her to continue when the timing is right.

Focus on teaching tenacity while the lessons continue, even if it's not easy. But the key is, once the child has completed a season or stretch of lessons, and she doesn't have a natural talent, move on. It's the reason that when kids pursue acting, the prospective agent asks to speak to the child alone without the influence of parents giving verbal and non-verbal cues. Acting takes a particular demeanor and is hard work. When they speak with the child, it comes through easily if he does not want to be on television or movie set when he is apart from his parents. Agents have one time to get it right, and they don't need a kid who has a bad attitude. It gives the talent agent a bad reputation and taints the child actor for future projects.

Have you ever heard a story like this about unfortunate circumstances? A high schooler who was homeless had not only social challenges surrounding school attendance, but many other nuanced obstacles such as lack of access to materials and space to study. Despite these hardships, this student made excellent grades and received a full-ride scholarship.

To the contrary, many times a privileged child who has all of life's resources doesn't apply himself in school and has the outcome to match. Why? In the end, the child must have determination to succeed. As a foundation, he must have the natural ability to like the task enough to excel. This is something possessed inside. In a 2019 scandal, actors allegedly paid for their kids to attend ivy league schools. This type of bribery and unfairness has likely existed since organized higher education has developed. Unfortunately for these overreaching parents, the costly means to buy their child's way into a school doesn't ensure academic success. These parents are wasting time and money. Not only are they not helping their kids, by giving them unearned "helps," they are teaching children that they don't have to work for what they want. These parents are better served to let their kids choose their own college and use personal contacts to jumpstart the kids' career paths in their first position.

I always tell kids to make good choices. As humans, our common thread is that everyone has freewill – freedom of choice to make good or bad decisions. To give an example in the extreme, people who are raised in abusive households make a decision to either imitate the abusive behavior or become the polar opposite.

It's possible for them to seek counseling to break the cycle, thereby diverging from the path that would unfold without any intervention. Inaction can also feed those traits (to which the individual may have some genetic predisposition), heightening them through a series of relationship experiences, thereby reinforcing the negative cycle. Luckily, the same holds true with kids and business. If the child is naturally gifted in sales or has a knack for a skill set, you can feed that instinctive or natural ability. You have yourself a potential business owner to hone.

To expand on the idea that we are born with many instinctive qualities while others can be developed, I'll give the example of my child's personal business experience. My daughter had her entrepreneurial start at the age of 15 selling products online and at shows. At the time, she had no idea she was capable of being a business owner. However, she is naturally creative and channeled this into her business. Although she was a procrastinator in school, I understood that she thrived in creative spaces and knew she could use this to her advantage. Being a business owner gave her that creative space, and she even decided to enlist her best friend to go into business with her, forming an LLC.

She added dimensions to this business by keeping her base in the creative element, which enabled her to then add skills that were outside her normal comfort zone, because we focused on her individual talents. Using the right foundation allowed us to open doors to entrepreneurial characteristics that were not part of her in-born traits.

Some of what occurred as a result of this undertaking was surprising and encouraging! While nothing challenges an existing friendship more than adding the business component to the mix, what happened was delightful. The two friends encouraged each other and shared day-to-day responsibilities. They planned events, visited wholesalers to select merchandise and placed items on their website. They used personal interests in the array of responsibilities to decide how to split up the work. They worked together with ease, realizing each other's strengths and weaknesses.

A good partnership is one where partners understand what their counterparts bring to the table. One was very good with the details, so she placed items on the website and photographed the merchandise because it needed to be done with care and meticulousness. The other partner set up live displays at shows and festivals.

There's no one single quality that will ensure success as an entrepreneur, but knowing what you're good at can help enormously. Many qualities can be taught, and the child will be better for it. Not only that, but the process of developing that future business owner can be taught, hence this book.

The longer my daughter ran her business, the more confidence she developed. No other kid in her school owned a business! By developing her strengths during this time, she learned as a teenager what it takes some adults a lifetime to recognize. She was reaping real-time rewards that no one her age gained.

This gave her the ability to see more clearly how she could excel in her endeavors. Those things she is good at become "the business," and the weaknesses were handled by a partner or outsourced by hiring someone else to do it. They dissolved the business in two years' time, but I congratulate her, as many lessons were learned through that process. My daughter has taken those lessons to heart and is still a business owner. Job well done!

Returning to the debate of born versus bred, there are some instances where a child's skills or special gifts show up quite early. Because kids are typically introduced to certain activities before liberal arts, parents tend to recognize talent in extracurricular sports, dance, gymnastics and musical instruments easier than some other equally expressive skills such as engineering and science. We need to recognize primary gifts early so we can be supportive to help develop and nurture them. Similarly, with entrepreneurial skills, it's not as easy to immediately see these qualities unless you are carefully watching. One would typically be more apt to notice a child showing athletic quality, if you see that child continuously score goals, as he appears to be highly advanced over other players his same age. Think of that scene: everyone is cheering – a parenting "light bulb" goes off because you have found something that clicks for your child; at that point you would put the development of those skills into overdrive. Because of the care you have for your child, you are an asset in developing skills that you recognize.

That type of audience is just what we need for our leadership and entrepreneurial development! How would one simply naturally notice this aptitude with the gravity it deserves? Is there a league for this, a class in school to take? No, but taking the path "less traveled" will lead to more real-life applications, where children are being shown both hard and soft skills that they will use later on in life. This is compared to solely learning how the soft skills may be applied later, such as in teamwork for extracurricular activities.

Again, it is more difficult to recognize cognitive skills because unlike athleticism, those are largely unseen. The trick is to know what to look for, and once you recognize them, to know how to develop them to their fullest.

So, we must study the skill sets of entrepreneurs. Once you know those qualities, then you can hone them and your child can really take off. They will forever see themselves in a new light. Remember, faith is the substance of things hoped for, and the evidence of things unseen. Translation: you may need to have a little faith to see the basis for the great things your child will be able to do in life! Don't take for granted the negotiating skills she exhibits with her little brother in getting him to play dolls with her, the spatial calculations he has to do to make the most monumental dominoes tower your household has ever known, the critical thinking she has to use to convince you to buy the latest video game. Any one of these could be the pillar for your child's success in life.

• TIP •

Ask your child who does she like or admire to give you an idea of her values and aspirations.

## Chapter 9
## Lessons Learned in Business

> *"Failure is simply the opportunity to begin again, this time more intelligently."*
> Henry Ford

Every person has age-appropriate challenges, and it's important to develop problem solving skills early in life, as these will be prolific during adulthood and in business. Kids, too, can practice critical thinking and become great problem solvers. When a child is faced with challenges, he can be conditioned to look at the problem, determine possible solutions and act on the solution.

This is great, because a business owner must come up with daily solutions to keep the business running. Moreover, if he can do it on a small scale, he can do it on a large scale, too. I taught my children at a young age that they have the power to make good choices; this becomes more critical as they mature and the consequences of their decisions become increasingly heavier. One bad decision can also alter the trajectory of one's life. Teens can lose scholarships, have a car accident, have children at an early age, take drugs; all of those things start with decision-making.

As adults, we must also be reminded about peer pressure. We will not always be there for our children to make decisions for them, and outside forces will entice them to do things we know are not in their best interest. Having a wealth of life experience on our side, we understand that certain decision can change the course of one's life, so it's very rewarding to know you have raised a critical thinker.

Being able to "play the movie," as Dr. Henry Cloud states in 9 Things You Simply Must Do, means an individual is able to forecast how one decision may give way to a chain of events, and put it all into context to see what this will mean for them. A child who can reason and understand there are consequences to every action may weigh the options and decide if the next action takes them closer or further away from her goals. At its most basic, the process of problem solving involves weighing the consequences, understanding the problem, determining a solution and acting upon that choice.

To clarify, here's a scenario. Your teenage son is at school for an after-school student body meeting. A smaller group of friends decide to leave school and take a quick ride. They ask your son to join them. "No harm in taking a quick ride," one mentions. The smell of marijuana is pungent and the driver looks less than coherent. Critical thinking ears perk up and your son begins to analyze the situation to weigh the possibilities.

If he gets in the car, there are various ways this could play out. One is the driver and passengers could be just fine with a simple joy ride. Unfortunately, other scenarios could occur, including being pressured to take drugs. Taking ownership over his choices in this scenario means not putting his decisions in the hands of someone who doesn't have his best interest at heart, or the cognitive ability to make those decisions on his behalf. He has a baseball scholarship to a state university already on the table, and might not fully understand each consequence. But he might have a sense that hanging out with these friends could detract from his goals.

Now, even more information is given to him if the driver was speeding through the parking lot with no seat belt, loud music and he was able to detect marijuana when the car rolled up. Now, a police officer could smell probable cause from a good distance. I learned that a charge – not a conviction – but simply a charge of drug possession many times means all scholarships are lost. A child could merely be present in the car, not smoke anything, and possibly lose the results of four years of hard work. That's right… not worth the risk.

Just as an entrepreneur who will no doubt face moral dilemmas, a child business owner will also gain those important gifts via choices like these. The business needs to be seen as honest, upright and customer-service friendly. For example, if a customer who wants to make a return of their purchase is in the wrong and there is no return policy for refunds, your child would be in their total right to refuse.

However, the child could also "play the movie" of what can happen when unsatisfied customers get too loud. And the negative ones are usually the loudest. Or even in the case of a dispute with competition. Your child might have a prior relationship with a customer and a competitor could do something morally wrong by trying to spread false information about the business so as to steal away that customer. Might your child want to do the same when the time comes around to "even the score," or would she want to maintain her integrity? Settling the score could gain one customer back, but what about the future reputation of the company?

Reaching too far for that one customer could cause her to lose more customers in the future. Retaliating could also cause the competition to become even more aggressive. She has to know that other customers will come along, and in the end, anyone who cheats will not prosper (and even if they gain the money this time, there is likely a horrible ache in their hearts that won't leave until they resolve their issues). Simply responding to falsehoods with poise in this case seems to be the order of the day.

Sometimes in business and in life, protecting yourself and your dreams means removing oneself from the situation before it becomes critical. I hope when your kids are faced with a difficult decision, they will be able to hear your voice saying, "Make good choices!" Because of the entrepreneurial qualities that you are helping your child develop, they can make definitive decisions without feeling as much pressure from others because they are self-leaders. To practice this, help your child make decisions on his own and come to his own conclusions without the telling him what they should be. Your child will become self-reliant with the confidence gained through this process, and he will know you are confident in his abilities, too.

We have seen examples of the overbearing parent who makes all decisions for the child, and they are surprised when the child can't accomplish a simple task or they go to college and get completely out of hand. As your child comes into her teens, she should be given greater responsibility to make her own decisions using tools learned in other areas, not just in the entrepreneurial areas. In the case of the helicopter parents, the child was smothered and protected to the point of suffocation up until college when they are thrust into independence, and they flounder.

Start early so that children are free to make age-appropriate decisions, and that will just continue as the gravity of decisions grow later in life. The practice of problem solving remains a theory until kids can see it unfold in their own trial and error. A further step in making good choices is recognizing not only bad ideas but also good opportunities.

• TIP •

Ask your child what they like most about being a business owner.

## Chapter 10
## Work Ethic

> *"There's no substitute for hard work."*
> Unknown

Successful people know that hard work is paramount in business and life. Daymond John states that entrepreneurs must be the best at their business or craft in his book, Rise and Grind: Outperform, Outwork, and Outhustle Your Way to a More Successful and Rewarding Life. Being the best means doing it well and doing it often. In addition, making it your mission to know all there is to know about your business makes you the expert.

There's another book called Outliers, in which Malcolm Gladwell states amid some controversy that being at the top of any field takes 10,000 hours of practice. The key, though, is that you use deliberate practice to stretch your skills to the limit day after day to keep moving forward (to note, strategies to remain competitive are many times industry specific). I will go further to say 10,000 hours are needed to achieve mastery not just in any business industry, but in any endeavor of life including sports and activities. Surely, in the unscripted world of an entrepreneur, one must always be evolving.

The value of hard work can be taught effectively in the immediate family when kids see the hard work of their parents, siblings, aunts or uncles. They begin to make associations after witnessing the fruit of the family's labor, knowing that hard work equals results. Unfortunately, reality TV is counteracting what children today are seeing in person and presenting, well, an alternate reality.

Famous-for-being-famous housewives, bachelors and social media mavens are portrayed in a way that makes it seem as if all things in life are easy to obtain; just post, tweet, pose and good things happen. This is so far from reality; these shows are often over-produced and the stars have every incentive to present their lives how they are not, since their fame depends on their image. Invisible to the viewer is the daily grind and a demonstration of what it takes to accomplish massive goals.

I love reading autobiographies because they are a testament to the personal hustle and triumph. Everyone has a story; everyone experiences difficulties. If they say otherwise, it's a lie. No one is exempt from life's challenges, but the difference depends on what one will do to change the situation. Your work ethic and commitment create the secret sauce that gives you an internal locus of control, the impetus to change your circumstances. Any worthy goal takes work: going to college, getting a job, establishing the career, reaching championship levels in a sport, buying your dream car or house, developing a business or raising a family. Every single task requires hard work. You cannot and will not avoid work. Therefore, take each opportunity to be a good example of hard work, dedication and commitment. You will be glad to watch your child reap the rewards.

### • TIP •

Share stories with your child about people who he admires and research together how his heroes' hard work resulted in success.

## Chapter 11
## No Fear

> *"Fear is faith in reverse gear."*
> Napoleon Hill in Think and Grow Rich

Fear is a topic that has far reaches in our lives, if we let it. This could be an entire book on fear rather than just one chapter – but as our focus is on action, we will include some extra tips to combat the statue-like effect that fear sometimes presents. We've talked some about viewing fear as misdirected apprehension. Did you know that nervousness and excitement are chemically identical in the brain?

If a reporter asks an athlete, "Did you feel nervous?" more times than not, the athlete will reply, "No, I feel excited." You see, these athletes have had some training and know something that we may not. They know how to turn their nervousness into excitement. Any goal worth achieving has the potential to make us fearful if we don't train our brains to think differently. What does that mean? It means we care about it. It means we are on the right track!

Fear is a short word that has a huge impact on our hearts and minds. My favorite scripture is 2 Timothy 1:7, "God has not given us the spirit of fear, but power, love and sound mind." Fear creates self-doubt and causes your brain to fill in the blanks of an emotional hesitancy with untruths about why you cannot carry out your intentions.

You are NOT in control if there is fear; fear makes you powerless. Fear can stop you in your tracks, prohibiting movement and progress. Your sense of self-efficacy is blocked; you no longer have the power or ability to envision accomplishments, because the fear is causing such apprehension. As we get older, due to our inhibitions, we may not verbalize that we are fearful, but our actions (or our non-actions) exhibit our fear. It takes much more effort to be fearless. It's easier to be fearful, because fear gives one an excuse. Fear provides reasons why you can't. Wading through water upstream takes more effort and energy.

People must alter their lives when removing fear and acting on their intentions. A hard look at what fear can do to a person comes in the example of when the abuser wants the victim to remain in fear. It's very effective for the person in power. Once they instill fear and have secured their victim, the abuse tends to escalate.

The victim becomes afraid to leave, afraid to tell anyone –and afraid to do anything that will anger the abuser. Fear is the motor that keeps the abuse cycle running. Once the abuser realizes the victim is no longer fearful of what will happen and seeks help from others to get out of the situation, the powerful hand guiding all actions of the abusee dissolves. A shift occurs so that the "victim" is no longer a victim. Ironically, we aren't born with unhealthy fear; we develop high inhibitions with reasoning. It's the reason children will jump in a pool, touch a hot stove, stick something in an outlet or cuts their own hair. No inhibitions.
The beauty of helping a child start a business is that fear hasn't been developed. Kids are bright-eyed and optimistic. They don't have the cognitive pathways set which immediately doubt the chances of success before a beautiful vision can unfold.

As critical thinking mechanisms progress, especially if children go through adolescence without experiencing success and accomplishment, thinking "more" about the chances actually means more doubt. Kids have no reason to believe that their lives can be anything but happy. It's only when you become older, develop a predilection for higher-brained thinking that these doubts creep in more frequently. More mental capacity for this type of higher-brained thinking (which can be quite incapacitating, ironically) can mean you land first on what you can't do. This is the opposite of what we want!

In other words, for all of us there areas of "slow growth" that we will try our best in, but will never come easily or naturally and therefore should not be a focus. However, when we gain more responsibilities as an adult, we experience overwhelm and have difficulty parsing it out.

That overwhelm likes to live in a place of fear, a place of insecurity. You first have the emotional response, and then your brain tries to assign meaning to it – even if it makes a huge error when you tell yourself the bad far outweighs the good. Then, the so-called "cannots" are hugely magnified. We end up focusing on them, having anxiety over them (when we should simply be outsourcing them). Focusing on our goals, our innate talents and finding our motivation, instead of our fear.

The proclamation about fear in this book is that we will not let fear undermine us or destroy the path of our lives, and we will teach our kids the same. Don't let your brain bully you!

Think about it – if you are in an abusive relationship, the abuser knows that fear is the reason you won't get out. There is a reason you may not reach out for help. There may be a reason why the victim tells themself that they can't get out of the situation. Money, the kids, that they love him/her, they have been convinced of their worthlessness and therefore will have no options without the abuser. The truth of the matter is, they have allowed the fear to convince them that any of those reasons are the things holding them back.

Habits and brain pathologies can take a huge effort for one to break. There can be a lot of shame associated with admitting the abuse has been occurring and getting to a safe place. Just this one thing alone can be enough help a victim maintain that it's "not really that bad." And the fear is just an accelerant added to that fire each time the abuse cycle continues.

One must start whole new brain pathways to stand up and say, "I trust in my own abilities to get out of the situation and I deserve for good things to come into my life." This happens in the face of the teaching that this person does not deserve any better. Many times, fear helps our brain choose the path of least resistance, and the familiarity of the situation makes it seem easier.

We can think of our collective nay-sayers throughout our upbringing as something called the "generalized other" which also helps us to form a bully in our head. Now, the best way to prevent this bully from forming in the first place in the brain of the child in our lives is to replace that space with something good!

The bad won't matter as much as you work on successes. If you learn one thing from this book, know that you must teach your child not to be fearful of what they want in life. Not to allow the reasons why "they can't" be a reason at all. There is nothing on earth that can stop you from achieving your goals and objectives. This is what athletes are told at the very start of their training. You can achieve whatever level of success that you want. The best coaches in the world tell you, "I don't want to hear excuses. You are not allowed to live in fear." Because if you're not afraid of what could happen, you won't talk yourself out of making something happen. It's so important to instill those qualities in a child to she will be able to say there is nothing dictating that you cannot do something. It does not excuse poor planning, not following through or not arming yourself with the knowledge of how to start, grow or expand a business. That's not what we're talking about; we are talking about simply not doing it at all out of fear.

• TIP •

Tell a child it's OK to be afraid, but it's more important to face the fear. Ask, "What's the worst that could happen?"

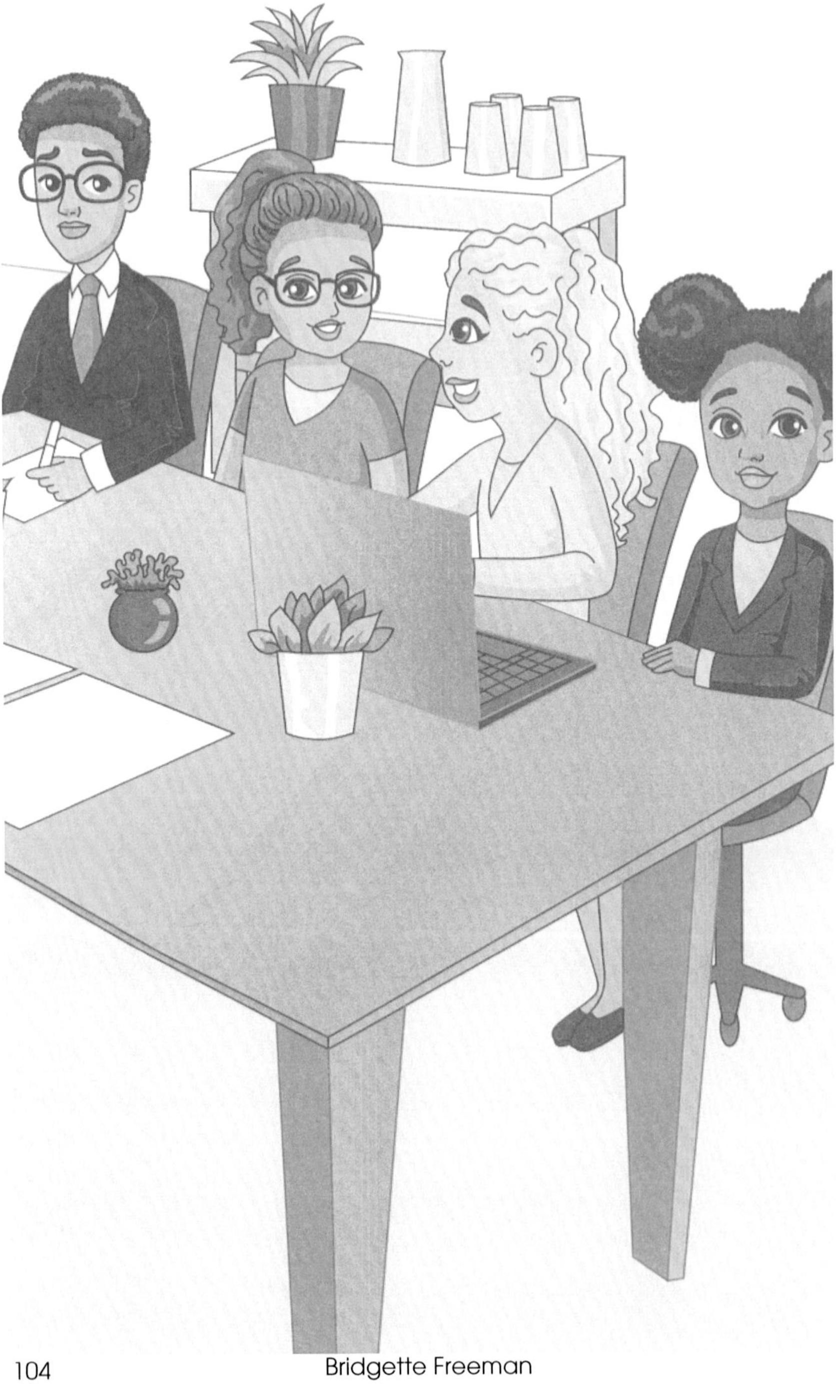

## Chapter 12
## Problem Solving

> *"Every problem has a solution...*
> *you have to be creative enough to find it."*
> Travis Kalanick

As we learned earlier, there is a constant debate on whether entrepreneurship-leaning attributes are born or bred. What we know for sure is that everyone is unique, and every person has talents and gifts. A child could have an innate propensity to have an enterprising attitude; you would be able to witness this in the flow of ideas from him. In other cases, skills of entrepreneurs are instilled over time, with repetition and the modeling present in being raised around other business owners.

Children that haven't experienced business ownership can be taught business skills. There are innate talents in every person, and signs will be present when you see her managing all her blocks and books in an orderly manner and fitting seemingly unrelated objects together like a puzzle. You'll know she will be a whiz at managing all the various parts. While your older son, who is always trying to make others laugh and convincing the neighborhood kids to take up a project to build the biggest skateboarding ramp that Elm Street has ever seen, may be a natural salesperson. Some skills are innate; you will seize and encourage them to flourish. Then you develop the others that are necessary or find a workaround.

Problem solving is one of those skills that you want as part of your child's arsenal. While some children are born with more determination, taking on a higher and higher order of challenges to solve throughout childhood is a great area for guidance and encouragement with the right mindset. You have the opportunity on a consistent basis to have teachable moments. Children will learn that in life, cause and effect means every action has a reaction.

I remember one time I decided to dye my own hair as a teenager, and my mother taught me a valuable lesson. She said something like, "You have never dyed your hair, nor do you know how, but if you are determined to do it, then go ahead. Realize that your action will have a reaction, it could be good, or could be bad." So, she let me exercise my own decision making. I preceded to do so with a homemade concoction that I had heard about. The project was a disaster, my hair was flaming red, and I wore the results of that mistake! I washed it four or five times, desperately hoping that some of the mixture would wash out. My hair was stripped of moisture and my preemptive venture into the hair styling world was very public. That action had a reaction, and I didn't forget that lesson.

There are age-appropriate lessons for kids of all ages. When my son was three years old, he was fearless like most boys. I would tell him that we don't have time to go to the hospital, hinting that he was probably going to get hurt, knowing that he associated hospitals with the stitches and staples he received by the prior year after a couple of unsuccessful feats.

Anytime he was trying his latest trick, I reminded him of this. It became clear to him that if he tried something dangerous repeatedly, it would most likely cause an accident. Through a lot of repetition, he got the message of associating the dangerous action with the reaction of going to the hospital (of course we would rarely not really take him, so I said this mostly in jest).

He knew in his little 3-year-old mind, 'If I decide to jump off this wall or jump over something and miss, we will be at the hospital for hours and pain would be involved.' This knowledge even had an effect on others. The daycare provider told me that when the kids were rough-housing, my son told them to be careful because we did not have time to go to the hospital! The daycare provider could not stop laughing because she could not believe that a toddler knew the correlation between a dangerous activity and the possible injury or harm caused, as tempting as those activities can be.

We all have that inner voice. However, both children and adults sometimes miss those important cues to listen to that intuition. Those hairs that stand up on the back of your neck when facing something that could cause harm is your inner voice alerting you to pay attention to something. Once you recognize those intuitive feelings, you can make decisions with confidence. Don't misunderstand, not every decision will be easy for kids; the right path is rarely the one with the least resistance. It is a parent's hope that their child will be able to make good decisions at a moment's notice.

Because peer pressure can be at play, kids do not want to look as if they don't know what they are doing. There isn't enough time to "think it through" if they are to maintain their air of security in the relationships that are causing them to question these choices. That's why one must rely on this instinct. The amygdala, which handles situations where you sense danger (which can be on a social level as we vie for status and pecking order as a means of survival) works much faster than the cortex where you think through situations.

The amygdala also directs where memories of past experiences are stored. When danger is sensed, both this "fight or flight" and the reasoning center are activated. But the amygdala is the region that starts the adrenaline hormones which first alert you to the fact that you are having an intuitive feeling, and if you learn to ignore this, you reinforce negative pathways in your brain. You must learn to tune into this intuition.

Regarding our example about the teenager who has a scholarship on the line and a decision to get in the car or not? The fear that activates that fight or flight response comes from the knowledge that a decision like this can change the course of his life. Being a quick decision-maker gives a child a sense of confidence. You can also teach your child that it can be important to take a step back, that way they can use more faculties to make a decision. You can say yes, no, or you can hold off on a decision as well. You want your child to be a problem solver and a critical thinker, which can help them along way healthy adulthood. The journey is also different depending on the sex of the child.

When my daughter was a teenager, I reminded her every day that she has the power to make good choices. The problem-solving process happens by first identifying that there is a decision to be made, then evaluating the cause and effect of things and deciding what is in line with your goals, values and life path.

Let's say a young woman meets a young man and he seems very nice. They exchange numbers and start dating. Over a short period of time, he begins to call and text her all the time. If she doesn't answer, he calls again or decides to come to see her in person. The young woman who may not have experienced this before thinks, 'Oh, he's so concerned about me.' His asking constantly, "Where are you, what you're doing?" – again, not unusual.

The problem comes then when he begins to text you back to back or call you 5, 10, 20 times if you don't answer. She might continue to think it's cute, saying to oneself, 'He likes me so much – he can't live without me.' However, that is a dangerous thing to believe. He can't live without you… that speaks volumes, and someone being obsessed with your whereabouts? They are thinking of you as a possession, not a person whom they respect.

It is not cute to receive 30 texts and 20 voice messages. When they can't reach you by phone, they start calling friends and relatives looking for you, searching places they think you might be. Not the least bit cute; this is scary behavior and should be treated as such. The situation escalates in every case, leading to something more dangerous. This happened with my daughter.

Although you think it could never happen to you or your child, you need to be conscious of those decisions your adolescents and pre-teens are dealing with all the time. You must discuss relationships with them and other social situations and check in with them on how they are doing, even if it feels uncomfortable. I thank God that she did not make the relationship more serious and therefore multiple times more difficult to exit. The experience made her much more skeptical and cautious about dating in the future. If your kids are confident in their surroundings, use problem solving skills to look at the cause and effect. They will make wise decisions.

Even if your son finds himself in a not-so-good situation, he can remove himself from the situation before it gets too serious and becomes critical. As my younger son matures, those life lessons continue to come into play. The cause-and-effect, problem solving skills and use of critical thinking to recognize opportunities are all important. For boys, the ego and testosterone can stir up emotions, causing impulsive decisions, so they have to be careful with that. Lessons about this are native to the process of a boy to becoming a man. If he makes a decision as a young boy instead of a man, it is one that will impact the course of his life.

When you teach your child cause and effect lessons that apply to entrepreneurship, those will also help the child to make definitive decisions while feeling less pressure in social situations. It's not that our kids will not make mistakes. It is not possible to raise a perfect child, teen or adult. In fact, mistakes are a huge part of learning. What my mother said to me about dying my hair was so impactful because she did allow me to make my own decision. In talking problems through when kids are young and helping them understand the gravity of their decisions and the fact that cause and effect exists, you help them form their own instincts. You will give them increasingly higher levels of responsibility in trying out their own decision-making starting from a young age. When they are toddlers, it starts with giving appropriate choices about what clothing they would like to wear, "A or B?" When they are a bit older, they can choose their own lunch. They can learn what it is to tell the truth and what it is to lie. For telling the truth about something hard, a reward can be given in hindsight so that they learn it is rewarding to do something difficult (but they should not know about this reward prior to making the decision). They can be given choices as to whether to share their bucket and shovels with kids in the sandbox, or not.

Your child was given the opportunity to choose the nature of the business in our entrepreneurial undertaking. All of these things build confidence and give him the fuel to tackle problems as they arise. He has ownership of the business, and so when an issue comes up, he knows you are there for support but that it is his issue to solve. The only thing you need to do is encourage him to keep going, not to give up when the issue arises (which you have done from when they were very small; it will be natural).

So when a child owns a business and must come to her own conclusions without a parent telling her to do so, she will be prepared. That process is so motivating and powerful as a lesson. It's the reason that children often say, "I can't wait to be an adult, so I can make my own decisions and do what I want to do." You're giving her age-appropriate opportunities to make decisions, so when she is a teenager, she's making those decisions from her own thinking process and not looking to another (say, an influence in her circle) with a blank look that says, "What should I do?"

Again, if they have no say in decision making through childhood, there is no independent thought process leading them as they branch out from the household. When they leave the home, they go buck wild and are self-destructive. It is where great (horrifying) reality TV is created; from a child that was smothered and protected to their detriment. They must have eyes on them all the time. When a child is finally free from that overprotective nature, they lose their minds. You don't want to give her a chance to respond in that manner.

If you give her some alone time, let her make some decisions and wait for her to generate some creative ways to solve a problem, then the theory turns into action. Let learning about decision-making be a positive experience on the stage of entrepreneurship, not one where the child feels as if they're drowning when they first get out on their own. Then her foray into adulthood will be more of a positive experience.

In other countries, business ownership is a way of life and provides many childhood lessons. I was talking to a Vietnamese gentleman who told me his parents and grandparents sold baskets. As a child in his family you would learn to weave, but he also learned other skills in the business, such as looking a person in the eye, asking how they were doing and listening to the answer. Only then would he proceed to ask if they wanted to purchase a basket. If they said no, he would handle the objection. Sometimes he could, and other times "no" meant "no." The point is, he was learning the sales techniques, creating the product, identifying potential buyers, clearly communicating with them and asking for the business.

In reflecting on other countries I had visited, unfortunately many of them were places that aren't as developed as the United States.

However, they are rich in how their children are reared. I am not referring to countries that are so destitute that they do not have access to clean water or food. I am speaking of countries that by American standards are considered poor. A large family may live in a two-bedroom home, but that does not mean destitution. Think about it. The child always has family around, they share food, clothes and stories. There's a close-knit feeling when you walk into these homes.

The children are grateful for the things they have, as they may be used to items being handed down, not new items. They aren't engulfed with technology. They use their imagination to have fun, play games and enjoy nature. At a young age, they learn the family trade and begin selling products that they know everything about. They possess self-discipline because the same tasks have to be done every day to be successful. Those skills make them self-sustaining adults. It's the reason that so many migrate to the United States and are successful; they apply the principles learned as a child and accomplish great things.

Entrepreneurial characteristics carry over to many other aspects of life. What I have learned from launching kids into college is that if you start the process of looking for scholarships sooner rather than later, kids can get scholarships for being an entrepreneur! If after trying different avenues, your child is not interested in having a business, still research what may apply to his particular interests. The same requirements that are needed for a business are applicable to running a non-profit organization as well. Plus, I always say that non-profit doesn't mean "no profit."

The same organizational skills for business are present in using critical thinking, relationship building and effective communication apply to non-profits. The impetus for a non-profit organization is a different than for, say, selling items online. If your child is not interested in creating a "business" so-to-speak, she may be interested in developing an organization that is formed for a cause. However, problem solving in starting a non-profit organization parallels for-profit businesses in many ways. You need a solid plan to start, you still will be looking most likely to raise money or support for a cause, however there is less emphasis on making it "profitable," rather, goals to help others are the primary aim.

The University of Iowa provides this list for growing problem-solving skills:

> **Step 1:** Define the Problem (You must first know that one exists!)
> **Step 2:** Clarify the Problem with details
> **Step 3:** Define the Goals; how does it impact your goals?
> **Step 4:** Identify Root Cause of the Problem
> **Step 5:** Develop Action Plan (Critical thinking)
> **Step 6:** Execute Action Plan
> **Step 7:** Evaluate the Results
> **Step 8:** Continuously Improve (This can prevent another problem from occurring)

Practice using these steps, even if it feels a bit cumbersome at first, in your child's everyday life. Ask him for three reasons why he has come to the decision he has in the action plan; it doesn't hurt to write this out, either. Can't seem to keep his room straight? Refer to the chapter on helping a child to complete chores. Then, once an incentive (positive or negative) is decided upon, and the child still struggles, have him go through the steps. He can reflect on why he is having an issue. Then, have him apply these steps when issues come up in business.

I was looking at a list of the top 10 scholarships for children under the age of 13, as well as scholarships for community involvement, and this brought me to another approach from a non-profit standpoint. If you can't get your child excited about creating her own business, getting her involved in community service is a win. As I mentioned in the beginning, some children feel a sense of entitlement that has to be undone by learning how blessed they are and how to be thankful is a process. Creating a non-profit organization or doing community service can open her eyes to other people's circumstances.

It's said, "You don't know what you don't know." If a child is never exposed to people who are in poverty, have a lack of education, lack proper housing, experience joblessness and even children just like themselves that are homeless, then they have no idea about realities of other people. Therefore, expose them to opportunities that will beget compassion, empathy and sympathy.

I personally don't believe in handouts, but I believe in a hand up. Meaning, I don't agree that society has the responsibility for someone else's welfare in trying to completely "save them." They need to learn to take responsibility for themselves. This all comes full-circle with teaching kids to become self-sufficient, forward-thinkers and not to be a continuous drain on their parents or society. However, I agree that everyone has a responsibility to help others along the way. Even those who have "made it" largely on their own (it seems to them), fail to realize that others have paved the way for them. It is unrealistic to think no one came before you, creating a path.

Creating a non-profit with a child will create a service mentality. All businesses provide a product or service. If you think about the premise of business ownership, the basic plan is to provide a product or service that fulfills a need, which means you have to learn to serve others. So the best for-profit businesses have strong parallels to non-profits.

No matter how big or successful you become in business, there is also always room for community service, so why not start there. Even larger companies allocate a certain amount of the budget for non-profit organizations and community service. Quite frankly, community fundraising or creating a non-profit organization is still making money, so it is great experience for business and provides just as much problem-solving expertise.

• TIP •

Teach a child to reason with a simple exercise. When going to grocery store, pick two items and ask the child which is the better deal, one 8-oz bag of chips for $1.99 or one 16-oz bag on sale for $2.49. Explain that you can get double the size for only 50 cents more and see that they understand it is a better value. They'll start picking it up before you know it!

Bridgette Freeman

## Chapter 13
## Develop Patience

> *"If a thing is worth doing, it is worth doing well. If it is worth having, it is worth waiting for."*
> Oscar Wilde

As adults, the gift of time shows us that things don't always go as planned. This is both true in business and in life as a whole. For example, an athlete training for the Olympics might start in childhood. The athlete makes daily deposits of sweat, hones his skills and most certainly gives up other things in childhood for his sport. He may prepare for more than a decade. A gymnast may start at the age of five or six by training, exercising, eating properly, stretching, practicing and competing locally and beyond.

The road to the Olympic gold medal is a hazy image at the edge of the horizon, but the goal is there, nonetheless. It takes a great deal of patience to stay the course and reach this monumental goal that so few accomplish.

Likewise, most business owners don't wake up, start a business and win millions in sales the first year. It takes time to build a business. The good thing is that a child does not have the same expectations and preconceived notions of success. Her success can be slow and gradual, delivering fruits along the way as she picks up skills. Your child is developing patience in her steady action. If she works diligently on the craft, she isn't focused on what she hasn't achieved, but what she is working toward. Help her to be patient and to learn from each experience thereby becoming better through the process.

The skill of practicing patience has a direct correlation to achieving goals. Once the goal parameters are set, the larger piece can be broken down into smaller continuous steps needed to hit each mark, as explained in previous chapters. Much like business, even writing a book requires a great deal of patience. This is the heart of one of the biggest applications from young entrepreneurship; the life lesson to help your child accomplish her goals in life and in business.

The advantage for kids is that his inhibitions don't occlude his judgment with the fallacy that the goal is too big or overwhelming. True, many folks in business might not reach their ultimate goals. But if you can catch kids in this impressionable period of curiosity and creation and him demonstrate to himself that his goals ARE achievable when approached in this powerful way, he is much more likely to fall into the category of those who do choose wisely and follow through to meet their dreams face-to-face.

However, this is an example of how you should teach your children to accomplish their goals. Any goal can seem overwhelming, but you have to decide if it is insurmountable. There are goals achieved with faith, determination and hard work.

As we reviewed in Chapter 7, The last parameter for accomplishing S.M.A.R.T. goals to ensure your chosen feat is T: time specific. There should be a time frame for the goal to be met. You determine the time frame. You are free to give yourself as much or as little time as you desire, as long as your goal outline is also R: realistic. Time is merely a marker in the sand that helps you to know that you completed the goal. If you have not met your goal by specified the time frame, then reset the time frame. Accomplish the goal with any new information that you have learned. For example, to reach the goal of completing the book, I probably reset the time frame three times. However, most importantly: it was completed.

Getting ready to publish, I didn't regret the time it took to complete it. I was simply proud of the goal achieved. Anything worth having is worth the work (and sometimes the wait). Your budding kidpreneur's experience is no different. The lesson is valuable and should not be overlooked. It doesn't matter how long it takes; the goal will be met at the right time. Of course, you wouldn't want to complete the first phase of business so many years later that the original business idea is no longer a need in the marketplace. So if the time frame is reset several times, it is also possible to take a look at why completing the steps was not a priority.

Perhaps there was an issue with some of the tactics that could be alleviated in the goal revision. Ideally, break up the goal into smaller parts to reach a complete whole. Oftentimes if the goal isn't achieved, it may be a life lesson to learn something more. Perhaps you learned that the market is asking for something else, and at times just a small tweak could allow you to step into this market.

Inventions are perfected when they don't work correctly the first time. The inventor does not give up, but goes back to the drawing board to address the issue with the product design. As a business owner young or old, take the time to continually improve your product or service. Sometimes this process takes practice. It's also good to have someone that you can bounce ideas off of to sharpen your idea. This is where a parent comes into play with the child. Kids can also be the other checks and balances. We know how brutally honest kids can be, so you could be assured they will be honest about your product or service. Help your child to use the information gathered so as to perfect her craft. Enjoy the process and remind your child to do the same. Develop patience, learn and grow in order to succeed. If your child becomes discouraged along the way, remind her that no goal is too great to achieve.

Help your child take the bigger goal and break it down into smaller steps. Doing so will help your child come up with a plan, or the "how," to accomplish the larger goal. This shouldn't stop after the first business; as a matter fact, it continues through to the next businesses your child may develop. One venture may lead to another. It is important to access accomplishments along the way, even when the goal has been pushed out some, which is another benefit to breaking goals down into smaller steps. There is a psychology to achieving the small wins first, giving way to motivation for accomplishing bigger and better things. It also helps one to stay humble and grateful for how far you have come. This can be compared to saving money. A common goal to undertake with a child is the purchase of a new fancy bike that may cost $150. You could break up the goal of saving $150 in one year to what needs to be saved per month to reach the goal. What must be done each day to reach a goal of saving $12.50 per month? Don't focus on end goal of $150; focus on the target at hand to reach the goal.

This makes it more clear to the child about what actions he must take on a daily basis. I give the same advice to real estate agents I have coached over the years. There must be consistent activity to result in the number of customers and sales desired per month to reach the yearly goal. Developing patience comes into play by implementing the process. The consistency in your execution of simple daily tasks to reach your goals comes from knowing and believing that the hard work will pay off. So, the crucial lesson during childhood is watching the metaphorical pennies drop in the bucket.

At first seeming mundane, after the child cashes in those pennies for dollars, then tens of dollars and then the full bicycle purchase price, the child can correlate the simple action with the final prize.

During this time of patience and work, keep the vision at the forefront of your mind. It's the reason vision boards are helpful. To make it age-appropriate for a child, it may include the latest game or device. Make the vision known. Every time the task seems to drag on, a quick look at the vision board can bring the jolt of excitement at the thought and the dream of that latest device. To remember just how fun it will be to play with and the laughs to be had with friends or siblings.

The process of making such a board tells the universe that you are expecting to accomplish these goals. After all, there is limited space on the board; choices must be made as to what he truly desires the most. This makes it more impactful. Great things happen when there's a flushed-out vision of the mountain climbed, the flag planted atop. Those things happen when forethought and patience exist to plan the trek and see it through. Webster defines "process" as a series of actions or steps taken. It takes patience to execute all those simple daily activities which complete the process.

My daughter competed in a local pageant. I remember the speech of the predecessor as she turned the crown over to the next title holder. The young woman read a story about a competitor who appeared in the same pageant and did not win the title for three years. Her grandmother advised her to stay the course and use that time to get better with each competition. Her grandmother reminded her that no matter the obstacle, that it was simply an obstacle to overcome. It was not permanent.

The emphasis was on being able to learn, get better and go back the next year with increased zeal and exuberance. In the story, the young woman reflected on how her support system didn't let her give up. Just competing at that level meant she was in many pageants before, and of course she didn't win them all. After showing up those first three times, she won the fourth time. Oh, how the patience paid off! She encouraged the girls that no matter the outcome, to persevere and be patient with the process.

If your child is not successful at accomplishing a goal that has been set the first time, this is the time to reflect on what the child could change; what was done correctly, and how could he have done it better? This reflection process is a part of life. There is not one person walking the earth that always had everything completely go his or her way. But if something goes awry, it's not the end of the world. It's only the beginning of a slightly altered path to accomplish the same goal. Ask him to be patient with himself during the process. Having patience is hard for most people, kids and adults alike. But it is necessary. There are good lessons to be learned in every step of the business process.

• TIP •

Don't confuse patience with mediocrity. No matter if you want to have a successful company selling widgets, or if you're an actor, you must keep in mind that the next project is part of a continuum. One project can build on another. One company's success can build on another. If one door closes, another can open – and if an opportunity continually does not seem to be working out, it's possible that it is just not the right time for that particular project. Patience is not the same as giving up. You follow your trajectory, and you return to the drawing board… or the vision board, as it were. Both patience with this process and the passage of time allow the life path to unfold.

## Chapter 14
## How Important is Credit?

> *"As parents, we teach our kids about things we feel competent in. That's why so many parents don't teach their kids about money."*
> Dave Ramsey

Maya Angelou once said, "When a person reveals themselves to you, believe them the first time." However, a person's words only give you 7% of the story, according to Mehrabian's rule. Correspondingly, when evaluating another person's character – whether for a business partner or for friendship – we look not just at what they say they will do. We would do well to focus on what we can observe from how they behave, as well.

A history of how they have handled themselves over time can also paint a picture of their character and beliefs. Compare this analogy to one's credit. A credit history gives a snapshot of how responsible you are with bills. As an adult, if you pay bills on time, it tells a future creditor that you will probably continue to pay their payments on time. Upon seeking appropriate licenses in your area for business, not only does one have a personal credit score, it's likely that your business will have a credit score, too. For simplicity, we will focus on the individual credit in this chapter, and the same principles apply to the business credit score.

In short, one's credit gives way to more buying power. People who make it a practice to build their knowledge of protecting money understand the value of good credit; in wealthy families, many times this knowledge is passed down to the next generation. Your credit score and history determine your interest rate on a house, car and insurance rates.

For example, if your individual credit score is low, it means bills were not paid on time or for the full amount due. Creditors take a deeper dive into public record items such as tax liens, bankruptcies and foreclosures – just to name a few. Furthermore, if your credit score is low, the assumed risk companies take on by insuring you or lending a mortgage will be higher. This brings you higher monthly payments.

For a car, alone, the price difference for the loan based on your rating could be hundreds of dollars per month. A car payment can be $350 or $650 for the same vehicle, depending on the credit worthiness of the individual. Conversely, the higher the credit score based on paying bills on time and not defaulting, the lower the rate to you as the consumer. If the loan interest rate is higher, you have lost real money because you are then paying more money over time.

So, if you add up the true cost of bad credit, it can be in the thousands. A 1-point higher interest rate for a mortgage means thousands of more dollars over a 30-year mortgage. Better credit equals a better rate and lower payments. Financing with a 1% rate versus a double-digit rate also makes a sizeable difference in the payment. The lesson: your bad credit will cost you, and that cost can be astronomical.

Pop Quiz: According to the algorithm for the credit reporting agencies, will they calculate a higher credit-worthiness rate for:

A) An individual who has 10 credit cards with low balances, or
B) A person who has two credit cards with high balances?

The answer is actually "A." The person with more credit cards! The credit reporting agencies view a person holding several cards with low balances as having more discipline than the person with two cards with almost all the credit tied up in debt. By the way, low balances are considered one-third or less of the credit limit. Therefore, on a card with a $1,500 credit limit, this means the balance should be $500 or less to help you maintain an optimal credit score.

Understanding this principle can help you and your kids to avoid heartache and, of course, save thousands of dollars. I implore you: save your child time and money by explaining the value of credit. Our children are at an all-time high in student loan debt.

The value of credit is usually not realized until one is knee-deep in debt, high interest rates and costly fees. It is stressful knowing that your payments are double what they could be… and less money paid goes to the actual principle with high interest. With great credit, you have more buying power. If a bank extends a line of credit to you, then you know have money for essentials if an emergency arises. You are then able to make more sound decisions on a day-to-day basis with this peace of mind.

Credit is a stepping-stone to creating a better financial future. With the newfound business, you need to help your child to be responsible with bills sent to your company. If services are provided to the business, you must pay within the prescribed time frame to remain in good standing. A wise business owner will effort to maintain both their individual and business credit scores. This creates the perfect scenario to develop and grow a successful business.

## • TIP •

Give the kid $5, telling him it is a loan and must be paid back. The payments will be $1 per week until the loan is paid off in 5 weeks. Then, do the exercise again explaining that after 5 weeks he still owes half of the money, because most of the money went to interest. I think most kids can understand why they are paying money back, but it takes much longer in the later example.

Bridgette Freeman

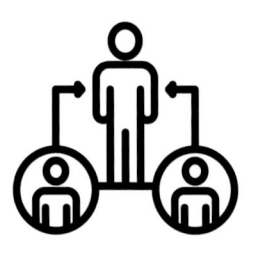

## Chapter 15
## Featured Kidpreneurs

> *"A star is born."*
> Unknown

The following kidpreneurs are some great examples of kids and young adults following their dreams. You'll see that they have listed someone as inspiration in their lives to help them along the way. That inspiration will come from you! They have chosen businesses that are interests of theirs. I hope you enjoy these stories as much as I did, and that they give you some useful information on how having a business has helped them grow personally and get to the next level.

### FAST FACTS
Name: Christian Robinson aka "Kindafye" and Dekori Robinson, CEO/Co-Founders
Business Name: **Defiant Ones Teen Magazine**
Find Us: Defiantonesmag.com
Age When Started: Christian, 16; Dekori, 17
Age Today: Christian, 16; Dekori, 18

*How did you start your business?*

The idea of starting a magazine came to us one night as we were sitting at the dinner table. We were discussing things we could do to inspire other teens to follow their dreams. In today's society, sometimes we are labeled as troublemakers. We planned to start a teen magazine that would defy all odds, have the same content as other magazines but also be unique. The uniqueness of our publication is that it is "For Teens, by Teens," and also highlights other teen and young adult entrepreneurs, entertainers, athletes, etc. We presented the idea to our parents, and once they saw how serious we were about this dream, they immediately backed it. Since then, we all have been working as a team super hard to create great content and push ourselves. Our goal is to get our publication into stores, airports, schools, juvenile detention centers, etc.

*Why did you start your business?*

We started the magazine because my brother and I have always wanted to work together and make an impact in the world any way we could. My dream is to inspire the world and become the best man that I can possibly be. In 2017, I created a clothing line called FYE Apparel, "Find Your Element" which encourages others to discover their true selves, passions, goals and motivations. This was created due to my being bullied in school and losing myself for a minute. But that wasn't enough for me! I wanted to find a way to constantly motivate the world and help others thrive as well. I think that this magazine is a great way to do it. My brother Dekori's dream is to show others that anything is possible, to simply put your mind to it.

*How did you come up with products/business ideas?*

The hardest thing was getting content for the magazine. Being new, you are competing with major magazines such as Seventeen and Popstar. We started contacting major artists letting them know about our platform and what we wanted to do. Thankfully Nova from So So Def's, The Rap Game winner of Season 3 – gave us the opportunity to share his story on our platform and was our cover artist! He gave us a chance even though we were new and though we were just starting out, he only did it all anybody needs his opportunities. We want all teens and young adults to know that is possible. People start supporting the magazine he started purchasing paperback copies since then we've created t-shirts and are setting up a big event. Details coming soon.

*How do you manage being a business owner and a student?*

It's hard, the workload of high school… maintaining all As and Bs takes a lot of effort. Drumline takes most of my spare time away, leaving me with the little time I have left in the day to build my business/brand. But I grew up watching my parents work through it and succeed every day, so I've become a great multitasker. It just takes drive and commitment. I use all of my spare time in the day to grow my businesses and grow as a person. The question you've gotta ask yourself is, "How bad do you want it?" My brother, Dekori, is on the football team as a running back, track team and is also doing a senior project on engineering. His schedule has been very hectic, so when he comes home and finishes all of his homework, he starts writing for the magazine and contacting people for us to feature.

*Who inspires you and why?*

My mother inspires me. Oleathia Robinson PKA "Butta B Rocka" is an international recording artist, bestselling author, playwright. In addition, she is CEO/Founder of Artists Rock the Mic, a nonprofit foundation that works with homeless college students. She says her biggest accomplishment is "us" and I've seen her turn down major opportunities for us, as well as touring all over the world doing major things which inspires us to keep going.

*What advice would you give other young people about starting a business?*

If you have a dream, of any kind… it is possible! Despite your current skills, experience, knowledge, et cetera…. If you want something in life, go for it! Work hard, learn from your failures/mistakes, always be open to opinions and believe in yourself. The world is yours, so take it. Create a business plan, know your target audience and keep improving. The biggest piece of advice I could give you is to start now. Start exploring your talents, dreams and passions; and make it happen; nothing is limitless to those who believe.

*What have you learned about being an entrepreneur?*

I've learned that it takes serious commitment and a great deal of passion toward whatever it is you're trying to achieve. You are required to put in hours of work daily and make sacrifices along the way to get you where you want to go. Being an entrepreneur for sure gives me an advantage in life, because I am so accustomed to hard work, dedication and multitasking now. I've become a better man by it, and I plan to do amazing things.

## FAST FACTS
Name: Amber Jewel Freeman
Business Name: **True Beauty Jewels**
Find Us: https://www.facebook.com/TrueBeautyJewels
Age When Started: 15
Age Today: 25

*How did you start your business?*

I am a woman who loves all things beauty, empowerment and singing! Every day is a runway for me, and my signature is that I dress to where I am going. I have always been creative, and my goal was to turn my creativity and skills into profit. At age 15, I absolutely loved jewelry and accessories. I also loved shopping, so my mom would drive me to the wholesale stores, we would purchase beautiful trending jewelry and then I'd set up stations at festivals and events locally. As I got older, I realized I loved fashion, music/singing and then empowerment to the point where I changed the direction of my business to cater to all my areas of interest. Now I've built my business as a beauty one-stop-shop!

*Why did you start your business?*

I started my business because I have a passion to see myself thrive in my sphere of influence as well as in womens' circles, alike. I wanted to start a business to showcase all of who I am. I never wanted to feel boxed-in. I am a recording artist, make-up artist, wig specialist, beauty guru, YouTuber, model and fashion stylist. I saw my true beauty in my shortcomings and hardships and desired to create a platform to share my story with others around the world.

*How did you come up with products/business ideas?*

I came up with products and business ideas by thinking about my own personal passions and how I can monetize them. For example, I enjoy changing my hairstyle often. I wanted to look different, but still protect and take care of my natural hair. So I decided to learn how to construct a wig. My first time trying, I wasn't even expecting to create a product or business. I was just trying the wig out to see how I liked it and it ended up being beautiful. I would be stopped in the mall by people asking who did my hair and how can they get the wig I was wearing, etc. Then that passion turned into a knack for hair coloring and creating custom wigs. I never expected my passions to take me as far as they have. When you are truly passionate about something, you will enjoy what you are doing and it won't feel like work, most of the time.

*How do you manage being a business owner and a student?*

I manage being a business owner and a student with one simple word: balance. I try my hardest to stick to a schedule and allocate at least one rest/self-care day per week. When I feel overworked or stressed, I'm not as productive, so having a day where I can relax or get a mani and pedi helps me stay balanced. A balanced lifestyle constitutes great success and happiness.

*Who inspires you and why?*

My mother is my biggest inspiration. She has a knack for business; growing up I learned so much from her. I watched her run two businesses, effortlessly. I think growing up with parents as entrepreneurs, I was able to see the not-so-glamorous parts of owning a business. It's tough, and sometimes entrepreneurs may not want to take on certain tasks or work when the rest of the world is sleeping. However, with determination and tenacity, they can succeed. My mom is like the superwoman of entrepreneurship. She is so passionate about her business and eager to pass her expertise along to others. It's one thing to be an expert, but an expert who's willing to share their knowledge with others is invaluable.

*What advice would you give other young people about starting a business?*

I would tell other young people to value and cherish failure and stay true to who they are no matter what happens. When starting a business, things will not always work out the first time and there will be a trial-and-error period. It's easy to question yourself when things aren't going as planned. Always trust your gut.

*What have you learned about being an entrepreneur?*

I have learned that there's power in believing in your brand. If you don't believe in yourself, then no one else will. I have had to take pride in my business even when things aren't going as planned.

# FAST FACTS

Name: Amara Leggett
Business Name: **A Young Legend**
Find Us: Ayounglegend.com
Age When Started: Blog about graduating high school and college (16). TEDx Talk, speaking services and book (17)
Age Today: 18

*What is your business about?*

My mission is to help young people discover their life goals and achieve success. This will be all while you build a brand and an audience that follows you wherever the wind takes you!

*How did you start your business?*

I started my business when I launched my blog to the world with a 99 cent domain name and a free website. I was the presented the chance to deliver a TEDx Talk, which launched my speaking career. Then, I released my book The Strategic Mind of a Young Legend to help people learn to leverage the resources around them to gain access to success.

*Why did you start your business?*

I started my business because I wanted to share with others how I graduated high school and college at 16. I knew that opportunities weren't being presented to people to excel in education, business and life. I became an advocate for higher education… but first and foremost, the right education.

*How did you come up with products/business ideas?*

I came up with the idea to start my business with my blog, first by understanding what resources around me I could use. I had no money, but I had the internet. I knew about bloggers who earned money, but most importantly gained an audience to influence. Being a public speaker came from understanding the business life cycle and how to continue building a brand when your accomplishments and audience grow. My book was really the cornerstone of solidifying what I knew and what I could provide to the world, as well as education about how to achieve the impossible in my readers' lives.

*How do you manage being a business owner and a student?*

I manage both roles by managing my time. I dedicate certain days and specific hours to my homework, work and business. If I have a day off from school, I catch up on business. If I need to respond to business emails, I do it while I'm eating lunch at school. When I am on break during my internship, I manage social media. I also use scheduling tools like Mailchimp, Later and Crowdfire to schedule posts and emails. I am on track to receive my Bachelor's Degree in Computer Science and buy my first property at 19 years old.

*Who inspires you and why?*

My friends inspire me! I have grown a network of young activists, entrepreneurs, and social influencers through social media that I have the chance to mastermind and collaborate with. If we are ever in the same area for business, we always make it a point to meet up.

*What advice would you give other young people about starting a business?*

My advice is to look around you and see what you can leverage. If you have a family member who owns a business, create a website for them and use that as your first client. If you have a camera, start a YouTube channel, or better yet, an account on TikTok since that is an upcoming platform that is pushing all content posted on there. We can get so caught up in the need for money to do anything. Hustle, hard work and a network can beat money.

*What have you learned about being an entrepreneur?*

I have learned that money and "overnight success" doesn't come overnight. It takes patience, hustle and consistency to make a difference. Learn to enjoy the journey along the way and build a tribe to help you get through it. I'm all about building a long-term legacy, which is something I realized I wanted at 14 years old. I'm here for the marathon, not the sprint.

## FAST FACTS

Name: Alejandra Stack
Business Name: **KidNewsMaker**
Find Us: https://kidnewsmaker.com/
Age When Started: 11
Age Today: 14

*How did you start your business?*

My mom was a full-time reporter. I was like 11 when I noticed they didn't have news about kids, unless it was sports or something. Well, she said if I wanted to see a change, "Be the change," and I got some friends and interviewed them. She liked it so much that she offered to help. I gave her $50 of my acting money to be my editor.

*Why did you start your business?*

To show kids real kids, not just celebrities.

*How did you come up with products/business ideas?*

I have lots of friends, and I know lots of kidprenuers (and

entertainment industry kids).

*How did you manage being a business owner and a student?*

I'm homeschooled, so it's manageable because I also act.

*Who inspires you and why?*

Honestly, my mom does. It sounds corny, but she's an award-winning journalist, and still manages me without any help.

*What advice would you give other young people about starting a business?*

Convince your parents that it's more than a hobby by starting on your own and showing them that you are serious.

*What have you learned about being an entrepreneur?*

That it is HARD, and you need a team. That there are haters, but you have to ignore them. And that you have to have a voice in it to keep it your own. You also can't be all about playing or doing it for clout. Have a purpose.

**FAST FACTS**

Name: **Robyn Gordon**
Find Us: www.robyngordon1.com
Age When Started: 11
Age Today: 15

*What is your business about?*

I am an author and anti-bullying advocate. I wrote my first book, Stop Bullying, at age 11. Today, I am a vibrant student and love to encourage my peers to make a difference when it comes to ridding the world of bullying. I am also the CEO of Next Generation Dance Team in Clarksville, Tennessee.

Business hats that I wear also include motivational speaking, worship leading and being a recording artist. I love to use my gifts to inspire the world. I have done several TV and radio show interviews and since releasing my first book, and have spoken to more than 15,000 people as part of my Anti-Bullying Campaign. In 2017, I also introduced my Stop Bullying 10-Day Course Curriculum for elementary school teachers to help school-aged children. I have shared my story with NFL Defensive End New England Patriots Trey Flowers, U.S. Senator Marsha Blackburn, Dr. Bobby Jones and Kirk Franklin.

*How did you start your business?*

I wrote the vision down, I showed my mother and we took it from there.

*Why did you start your business?*

I started my business after I had an experience which led me to write a book.

*How did you manage being a business owner and a student?*

Managing being a student, entrepreneur and volleyball player is tough, but it's all about time management. I go to school until 2:30, then until 5:30 I have practices. I get my schoolwork done after practice.

*Who inspires you and why?*

My mother is my biggest inspiration.

*What advice would you give other young people about starting a business?*

Go for it – because if you don't, you'll miss out on something potentially big.

*What have you learned about being an entrepreneur?*

I've learned how to be more responsible and how to be a young adult.

## About the Author

A graduate from Georgia State University with a Bachelor's Degree in Management and designations from Toastmasters International, Bridgette Freeman, affectionately known as B Free is a serial entrepreneur with corporate experience, an accomplished real estate investor, broker, speaker and trainer.

• NOTE FROM THE AUTHOR •

Our children are our treasures and gifts to the world. A child who understands business principles develops confidence, giving way to a willingness to take quality risks in other areas of life and many successes. These principles can be taught and nurtured as lessons that will be remembered for a lifetime.

As a child, I felt an ingrained sense of initiative and responsibility. I would come out with my apron and take orders as a pint-sized business owner of a "diner," preparing the food in the kitchen with care. Who knew, at my tender age, that I was "playing entrepreneur?"

I hope this book inspires, ignites and implores the reader to act. There are so many golden nuggets. It's not just a book, but a manual with tips along the way to implement and empower the children and young adults in your life and even yourself. Enjoy and be great!

To order this book:
**www.kidtoceo.com**

www.facebook.com/bfreespeaks

All social media platforms
@BfreeSpeaks

Thanks for reading! Please add a short review on Amazon and let me know what you thought!

You can place an order, make a request for a speaking engagement, book me for your next event or simply reach out with your questions and comments.

*Here's to more reading and empowering others!*